The
FISHING
HANDBOOK

Published by Sellers Publishing, Inc.
81 West Commercial Street, Portland, Maine 04101
For ordering information:
(800) 625-3386 toll free
(207) 772-6814 fax
Visit our Web site: www.rsvp.com • E-mail: rsp@rsvp.com

President and Publisher: Ronnie Sellers
Publishing Director: Robin Haywood
Managing Editor: Mary Baldwin
Senior Editor: Megan Hiller

ISBN: 1-56906-992-1
ISBN 13: 978-1-56906-992-9
Library of Congress Control Number: 2007925781

10 9 8 7 6 5 4 3 2 1

Conceived, designed, and produced by
Quid Publishing
Level 4 Sheridan House
114 Western Road
Hove BN3 1DD
www.quidpublishing.com

Illustrations: Matt Pagett
Design: Lindsey Johns
Printed and bound in China

NOTE
Every effort has been made to ensure that all information contained
in this book is correct and compatible with national standards at the time of
publication. This book is not intended to replace manufacturers' instructions
in the use of their products — always follow their safety guidelines.
The author, publisher, and copyright holder assume no responsibility
for any injury, loss, or damage caused or sustained as a consequence
of the use and application of the contents of this book.

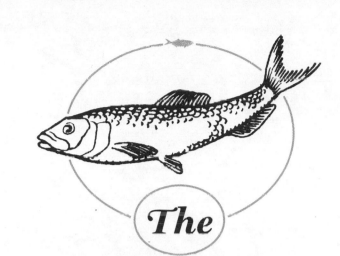

The
FISHING
HANDBOOK

An Illustrated Guide
for Anglers

Rob Beattie

SELLERS
PUBLISHING

CONTENTS

Predator fish love
lures — see page 46

Respect other anglers'
space — see page 21

It's your job to look after the fish you catch — see page 118

INTRODUCTION

Welcome gentle reader, to **The Fishing Handbook.** *On behalf of the management, I hope you have as good a time reading it as I did writing it. Come on in, sit down, and put your feet up — we don't stand on ceremony here. Although you can read it from cover to cover, this book has been designed for dipping, and whether it finds a place by your bed or in the smallest room in the house, it's all the same to me, so long as you enjoy it.*

So, you've wandered into a bookstore, picked this off the shelves, opened it to a few different pages, and read about ghosts and good luck, secret lakes and anglers' hats, homemade baits, fly tying, and what it's like to be a fish — and you're probably wondering what kind of a book this is supposed to be.

Well, I hope it's a guide in the truest sense, something that goes beyond the modern fishing manuals that are busy reducing the mystery of angling to a set of instructions and require nothing from the reader than the ability to follow orders. You won't find any of that in here. Yes, I'm happy to pass on the little knowledge I've accumulated in more than

30 years of fishing (I tend to think of it as dust collected under a bed), but there'll be no "do this" or "do that" — not while I'm in charge. Instead, I hope that you'll enjoy the stories here and that some may inspire you to try something new, or just to pause for a moment and think about why you go fishing and what it means to you.

For those readers who find my tales of the English countryside, her waters and her fish, a bit confusing, I beg for your patience and understanding. We are all anglers, wherever we pursue our obsession, and if there are some differences of detail between your fishing life and mine, there are many more experiences in these pages that we can share. We've all known the thrill of anticipation that waits for us at the water's edge, the bird's clear call at dawn, the thump of a large fish, food snatched between casts, the hand raised in greeting to another angler, the shiver of a lonely walk back through deep woods to the car. We share these things, and no matter where in the world we are, all anglers fish under the same sky.

See those funny little tufts where the river narrows and speeds up? That's hair torn from the frustrated heads of all the anglers who ever sat on these banks dreaming of the fish they were going to catch.

FOOD FOR THOUGHT

For one reason or another, I don't catch many fish. This leaves me a lot of time for thinking and, because of where I live, so tantalizingly close to the object of my obsession, these thoughts turn naturally to fish and fishing. Why should a grown man continue to pursue a hobby that he began so many years before? Where's the attraction? How many times can you catch a silver fish of a few ounces and put it back? How many times can you arrive so full of hope and leave so firmly put in your place?

I've been trying to answer these and other angling-related questions for 35 years, and this book is my first attempt to put down some of the answers. Like my fishing, it's a pretty ramshackle affair, but hopefully still useful for all that. It's certainly not a book of tips, apart from this one: If you want lots of instructions, buy another book. There are plenty of those, and plenty of magazines that will improve your catch rates, if that's what matters to you. Here you won't find too many pages on "bagging up" or where to go to catch the biggest this or that. I understand that people want to catch fish, but for me that's only part of the reason for going fishing — and not necessarily the most important part.

THE FISHING EXPERIENCE

That's why this book is populated by stories that some anglers may find puzzling or even out of place — ghost stories, luck, things you can catch that aren't fish, friends, myths, hats, empty nets, baits you can eat, cheating, provisions, first and last casts. To me, these stories are integral to the fishing experience and are at least as important as any fish I might catch.

A typical day for me — a quiet spot, a single rod, a few gentle ripples on the surface . . . and not a fish in sight.

My friends have unkindly pointed out that this is because I don't actually catch many fish and am therefore unfamiliar with much 21st-century terminology — words like "lunker," "stonking," "slab," "screamers," "lump," and so on. Just as Mozart was famously criticized by his patron Emperor Joseph II for including "too many notes," my fishing attracts the opposite criticism that there are "not enough fish." Which is nonsense — I'm sure I caught one last year.

There are plenty of stories, though. Good ones, sad ones, and — I hope — a few funny ones. And since this is my first pass at it, there are plenty of stories yet to be told. And plenty of fish, too, because the two are always deeply intertwined.

In the end, what I'm trying to say is this: Every fish comes with a story, and these are mine. You can read about them, and I hope you enjoy them, but in the end, if angling grips you as it does me, if it makes sense in a world where little else does, if you "get" it, then you will surely want to write your own.

WHY GO AT ALL?

If I had a penny for every time someone asked me why I went fishing, then I'd have enough money to buy an ice cream. It would be a very nice ice cream, because I've been asked by a lot of people, but there's no sense getting carried away. It's only fishing, after all.

I used to try and explain why I went fishing, usually at parties. I thought I'd got quite good at it. I'd tailor my replies depending on who was doing the asking. Guys got the huntin', shootin', fishin' reply — how it was all muscular and military, harsh conditions, gale-force winds, mighty battles, tooth and claw. Women got the I'm-so-sensitive reply, which stressed contemplation, reflection, long walks by cool streams, gazing meaningfully into the distance, a sense of duty bound and destiny — Aragorn in an anorak.

Now I can see where I went wrong: too much detail. Thoroughness was always my weakness — that and an inability to spot the early signs of a listener losing the will to live.

These days I don't bother. I look the questioner straight in the eye and reply: "I can't really explain why. Fishing's just one of those things that you either get or you don't." They can move on, relieved, duty done, and I can return to plotting how I'm going to get that huge bass out of the reeds next week, what bait I'm going to use, and whether or not I could get one of these mini sausage rolls to stay on the hook.

STOCK ANSWERS

Should you as an angler ever be pushed for an answer, there are some stock ones that carry enough weight to convince most people. You like the peace and quiet. It's a day out with the guys. It's something to do with your son that doesn't really cost any money. It gives you a chance to think. It gets you away (this must be said with a wink or rueful smile) from under your wife's feet. All of these are acceptable explanations that stand up to casual scrutiny, yet none comes close to defining the appeal of our watery weakness, the dark mistress of angling.

I've seen people treat it as if it were just another sport, and I knew that despite appearances, they didn't get it at all. I've watched it consume people in the way that a love affair does — especially an ill-advised love affair — seen them lie to their partners, sat next to them while

"So let me get this right. You just sit there all day and if you catch something then that's fine, but if you don't, then that's fine too?"

they phoned work, all weak and whiny (with perhaps the occasional cough), had them cry off from football to me on the phone with the same voice while the river chuckled accusingly in the background.

I've watched people survive that and make their peace with fishing, make it a part of their lives rather than placing it at the very center, and I've seen the occasional angler transcend and move to an entirely different place where they hardly seem to fish at all yet are somehow . . . always fishing.

GETTING IT

I'm not convinced I know where I am in all of this or exactly why it is that I go — and that's after 35 years (though I did have time off for good behavior when I discovered beer and women and rock and roll). I'm not a naturalist, though I can recognize a willow tree, a kingfisher, a cow, and a mosquito; and for someone who spends a lot of time seeking out their company I seem to have learned precious little about fish and their habits. The life of the water and its banks mainly passes me by, and I'm by far the worst predictor of the weather I know — I even treat my own advice with contempt. I'm barely technically competent, though I like to think I have a decent cast, and know only half a dozen knots, use about the same number of baits and probably fewer techniques.

And yet, and yet. To return to my standard party routine, I "get" fishing. It makes perfect sense to me. When people go through the whole "and you just chuck them back?" routine and look at me as if I'm mad, I know — deep in my heart — that it's they who are mad, not I.

Although it's undoubtedly the reason why most anglers go fishing, actually catching something substantial is only the icing on a particularly delicious cake.

GOING ON A WHIM

We could go together when this book is finished. There's a small river near here, barely bigger than a stream really, and November's not yet grown so fierce that a brisk walk and a hot mug can't keep out the cold. There may be a chance of a good fish at the big bend where the river widens and seems to draw breath — you can fish there if you like.

Me? I'll sit with you for a bit and watch. We can have a chat, and anyway, it's interesting to see how other people go about things. After that I may have a wander downstream, and I want to check how the old footbridge is holding up in these first winter frosts. After that, I'll see where the notion takes me. The cattle's water is usually frozen at this time of year, and walking in the footsteps of cows is always good for a laugh, so long as I don't fall in. Then I might snip a little holly from over by the gate. Who knows?. I may not fish at all.

THE ROD

Rods are very personal things. You can put several of them — made of the same material, with the same length, reel seating, and action — side by side, and one of them will just "feel" right. Like golf clubs (though obviously golfers lack anglers' subtle appreciation of nuance), every one is slightly different.

In the ancient days of fiber-glass rods, experienced anglers would recommend that beginners intending to start out bobber fishing get a rod with an all-through action (i.e. one that bends all through the rod, from the butt to the tip, rather than just at the top section) to use as a general-purpose rod. It's still pretty sound advice, but if you can find a rod with interchangeable tip sections to suit different needs, that's an even better bet. If casting lures, rather than float fishing, is more to your taste, you'll find that spinning rods come in a wide range of lengths and strengths, but it's not hard to find a general rod that will keep a beginner in fish for the first few years. Don't worry about getting lots of different kinds of rods for different kinds of fish — despite what the tackle manufacturers say. Rod collecting is every angler's disease, and you'll catch it soon enough.

Don't spend a fortune on a rod, at least at the beginning, because there's no need to. There are plenty of excellent all-purpose rods at a price that everyone can afford, and manufacturing techniques are so good that as long as you buy from a recognized tackle shop, you won't go far wrong.

Of course, if you've got your heart set on a particular kind of fish or style of fishing, you may be better off with a very specific rod. For float-fishing on a lake for trout, consider a long, fairly light rod of between 13 and 15 feet (4 to 4.5 m.) with a 1 lb. test curve. If you want to catch something bigger, such as carp, pike, or catfish, you'll need a strong two-piece rod of about 12 feet (3.5 m.) with a test curve of around 2 lb. 4 oz. A spinning rod for small trout can be fairly short and lightweight, but if you're after bass your rod will need to have some backbone.

TEST CURVE

What's a test curve? Imagine holding a rod horizontally with a reel on it and line threaded through the rings. Now, keep adding weight to the end of the line. When the rod bends to 90°, see how much weight it took — that's the test curve. (And yes, many rod builders believe this is the least worst way of defining the action of a rod.)

If you're just starting out, an all-purpose rod at a reasonable price is probably your best solution.

THE REEL

After the rod, the reel is the second most important piece of tackle you'll ever own. With even minimal care (like at least putting it back in its bag at the end of every trip), it will last for years. So which kind should you buy?

To my mind, the spinning reel is one of the most brilliant pieces of engineering ever devised. To take the concept of the traditional circular reel, rotate it by 90°, arrange the gears in such a way that you wind it as normal, and then provide a simple spring-based mechanism for winding line onto the spool and releasing it, is pure genius.

Spinning reels — closed- or open-faced — are the most popular type of reel around, and they are suitable for all kinds of fishing in all kinds of conditions. There's all sorts of weird and wonderful technology built into this kind of reel to keep the retrieve fast and smooth and to prevent line twist; you'll also hear a lot about ball bearings. My advice? Don't buy anything for less than $50 unless you're exceptionally low on funds. Apart from that, knock yourself out. Shimano make excellent reels; I still like the newer Mitchells (though I know some anglers don't); at the cheaper end, Okuma reels are superb value.

If possible, take your rod with you when you buy a reel so that you can feel it *in situ*, and make sure it feels balanced in your hand. Wind the reel backwards and forwards and try to spot any "wobble." If the reel feels like it's moving slightly from side to side, it's not properly balanced.

Spinning reels come with either front or rear drag controls, which allow you to adjust how much pressure the fish can put on before it can start taking line from the reel, even when the bail arm is closed. I don't have a preference between the two. If you're interested in catching pike or catfish, you'll probably hear a lot about "baitrunner" reels, which are designed to allow large fish to take line freely from the reel, but in a controlled fashion so it doesn't tangle and snap. Some reels also have very large-capacity spools, enabling anglers to fish at greater distances. A good reel will come with a spare spool, and it's worth buying a little bag to keep it in if one isn't included.

One final tip: don't overload the spool. Leave a gap of about an eighth of an inch from the lip. This will allow you to cast freely while preventing tangles.

Of all the types of reel available to the angler, the spinning reel is the easiest to use, as well as the most versatile.

The spool here is empty; don't fill it right to the edge with line

The bail arm wraps line around the spool when you reel in

Balanced handle prevents reel wobble

Rear drag can be adjusted to let fish take line

THE TACKLE

There's nothing an angler enjoys talking about more than his tackle, and if you had the money you could probably spend every penny on the latest this and the most modern that. But what do you really need to take fishing? Think about that and you won't go far wrong.

Aside from a rod, reel, and line (see pages 10, 11, and 39 respectively), you're going to need a landing net — at least we hope you are. Anglers who wade or ramble a lot often prefer to have a net that folds up so they can carry it on their backs. For more general use, choose between a triangular net for larger fish and a round net for smaller ones; all nets should use the newer soft "micromesh" rather then the coarse old-style netting.

Unless you're after extremely large fish, a telescopic handle is your best bet because it packs up small and is easy to carry. Only use the handle itself to lift small fish out of the water. For anything

bigger, adjust the net toward you until you can grasp the frame and lift the fish out that way. If you fish somewhere with high banks, you'll have to buy a second, longer handle — there's nothing worse than finding a fantastic spot only to discover you can't land anything from it because your net doesn't reach. As far as retaining live fish goes, I don't approve of keep nets, so I'm not offering any advice.

You should also consider an unhooking mat to protect fish while they're on the bank, and some sort of sling to weigh them in. To be honest, a large wet plastic bag does the job just as well for most fish, though very large catfish and pike deserve a proper sling. You'll also need a set of scales, and although some anglers prefer digital scales for their accuracy, these need batteries, so I go for a mechanical scale with a maximum weight marker so the weight stays recorded after the sling and the fish have been removed. If I need to measure a fish I use an old cloth tape measure because it won't do any damage to the skin.

THE TACKLE BOX
Always an angler's pride and joy, your tackle box can be an antique thing of beauty, a portable palace of technology, a buoyant, sophisticated den of deception, or, like mine, something you got free with

Many anglers enjoy the "kitchen sink" approach to tackle, and there's nothing wrong with that, as long as you have a stout bag and a strong back.

a magazine. No matter what it looks like, it's what's inside that counts — and what you do with it.

Being a great believer in simplicity, my tackle box usually includes only those items that I think are essential for my kind of fishing. These include:

+ a selection of barbless hooks from size 4 to size 16 (some people go as small as 22)
+ a small collection of traditional-style stick floats that suffice for both still and running waters
+ a selection of shot with which to weight the floats
+ some ledger weights of various shapes and sizes (my favorite is invariably the Arlsey bomb, a pear-shaped lead weight with a built-in swivel for attaching it to the line)
+ some plastic ledger stops
+ a few swivels.

The one item of tackle I'd miss if I left it at home would be a plumb — a weight with a bit of cork in it that you attach to your hook and use to gauge the depth of the water you're fishing in. For years I fished without one, guessing the depth in a haphazard fashion, but now I realize how stupid I was and consider it an essential piece of tackle.

Add lures and a few wire traces, scissors or line clippers, a pair of hemostats for unhooking, and you're pretty much done. Even then you can look on the fly anglers with envy, because they really know how to travel light.

UMBRELLAS VS. PONCHOS

We'll talk elsewhere about clothing (see page 78) and something to sit on if you're stationary for hours, but it's worth

Alternatively, here's my minimal set-up — rod and reel, blow-up cushion to sit on, tiny canvas bag, and a can of your beverage of choice.

mentioning umbrellas at this point. I consider them at best a necessary evil; they're heavy and awkward, and are just about bearable if you intend to stay in one spot for a long period of time in really foul weather. Given the choice (and assuming it's not absolutely pouring), I'd always rather use a simple waterproof poncho — it packs down into nothing, leaves your arms free, can be spread out to cover your gear and whatever you're sitting on, and if you know what you're doing it can even be pressed into service as a simple shelter.

Personal Favorites

There are no doubt hundreds of items of tackle that I've omitted to mention here, but I consider most of these unnecessary, faddish, or very specialized. Tackle is a personal choice, though. As you come to love fishing, you'll also come to love some bits of tackle more than others, and those will naturally take up most space in your tackle box.

TYPES OF FISHING

If you're completely new to fishing, it can be a bit baffling. It's bad enough trying to get your head round the concept of spending hours attempting to catch something only to put it straight back, but then it turns out that there's lots of different ways to do it and each style of fishing has its own tackle and techniques. Here, in two concise pages, is all you need to know about the main types of fishing.

BAIT FISHING

Bait fishing is probably the broadest church of all, since it includes everyone from anglers who fish for giant catfish and pike to those who pound out tiny panfish on long, wand-like rods. Broadly speaking, it involves a rod, reel, line, some end tackle to keep the bait on or near the bottom or floating at a specific depth beneath the surface, a hook (occasionally more than one hook), and something on the hook that fish like to eat (or that can fool the fish into thinking they want to eat it). You can bait fish anywhere and catch every single species of fish that swims in North American waters, from the smallest pumpkinseed to the largest sturgeon.

On still waters, the bait is left in one place for the duration of the cast, but on flowing water like rivers it can also be allowed to move with the current under a bobber, or twitched down the river bed. Although most bait fishing is static (i.e. you pick a spot and stay there for the entire session), some bait-fishing anglers like to move frequently, casting their baits into different spots, hoping to find the fish rather than waiting for the fish to find them.

Fishing with a fly is arguably the most sophisticated kind of angling you can do (according to those who go fly fishing, at least).

LURE FISHING

Here, anglers are after those fish that like to eat other fish as well as small animals and amphibians, so the object of the exercise is to present something that looks both tasty and weak so that the larger fish will snap at it. Tackle for lure fishing is simple: a rod, reel, line, and a lure (occasionally more than one lure). The angler casts the lure out into the water and then winds it back in, hoping that the combination of its design and the way it moves through the water will convince predatory fish to attack and hook themselves. With lure fishing, there's rarely any need for the angler to strike.

The lures themselves vary in size, shape, color, and texture depending on what they're trying to imitate, but all have either a single or treble hook hidden about their person — and sometimes more than one. Some are designed to mimic particular fish or other prey, while others — usually called "spoons" — attract predatory fish by reproducing the "flash" and vibration that a small silver fish makes when it moves through the water. Different designs allow lures to be fished at various levels in the water, depending on where you're fishing and the type of fish you're trying to catch.

FLY FISHING

Here the equipment is simplicity itself: a rod, reel, line, a short length of lighter line for the end, and a concoction of wool, feathers, fur, and other bits assembled round a single hook so as to look like a fly or other small insect. You can use flies to catch most species of fish (my friend Sean caught an eel on a fly once), but the usual quarry are trout and salmon.

Once a fly is cast into the water it's either left to drift naturally in the current or retrieved in such a way as to attract the fish. There are thousands of ready-tied flies that anglers can buy, but many enjoy the challenge of creating their own, and we'll look at that on pages 58 and 59.

Whereas you can pick up other kinds of angling pretty quickly, fly fishing offers a unique and more demanding challenge, especially to beginners. That's because there's no

Pole Fishing

This is fishing with a rod but without a reel, and is mainly suitable for catching smaller fish, up to about 5 pounds (2.25 kg.). In this style of fishing, the line is attached to a piece of elastic on the tip of the pole, which offers some extra "give" when you're playing a fish, and the fish is brought closer to the water's edge by removing sections of the pole and dropping them on the bank. Even though poles can be long enough to fish 40 feet (12 m.) or more out from the bank, the end tackle can be very light and delicate because it's being fished directly under the tip. This means there's no problem with wind or surface drag. Competition anglers love poles, but I've always thought they were a bit weird.

weight at the end of a fly-fisher's line. Instead, you use the weight of the line itself to cast, a bit like cracking a long whip (fly fishers are at this point holding their heads in their hands in despair, but there's much more detail about fly casting on pages 28 and 29).

It may not look much like a convincing insect to you or me, but as long as it's enough to fool a trout, even the most outlandish-looking fly will do the trick.

THE QUARRY

As a young angler, I always went fishing for whatever I could catch. However, as the days go by I'm becoming quite enamored of the idea that with a bit of thought and a bit of planning I can actually catch a specific kind of fish, rather than just chucking and chancing it.

My friend Ray calls this "knowing your quarry," and he has been convinced for years that it's *the* way to fish, while I have only recently come round to the idea.

Temperamentally I've always felt that the problem with going after one species was that, even if you were successful, it meant that you'd never catch any of the other fish. This always seemed to me to be a waste; a curious decision to close doors that were conceivably concealing large numbers of fish. And for me, it's bound up in the intrinsic tension of fishing. Despite the thousands of words I've written to the contrary, praising

A typical angler, disappointed at not catching the fish he was after, can usually make the best of a bad job and at least pretend to be happy.

true anglers as being those people who aren't measured by the number of fish they catch, I've actually always felt the opposite deep down. Indeed, I can never quite relax until I've caught something. It doesn't have to be anything very big, as long as it's *something*.

DIFFERENT STROKES

Even though we're now singing from the same hymn sheet, Ray and I still make an interesting pair. Ray goes fishing prepared for every eventuality to do with the particular species he intends to catch. Thus, he might take a couple of rods, two reels, lines and leaders of various strengths, a box of floats and weights, different hooks, baits, several kinds of groundbait, rod rests of three different lengths, two seats, half a dozen hats . . . OK, I'm kidding about the hats, but you get the idea.

The last time I went fishing, I took all my tackle in a woman's zip-up purse that I bought at a yard sale for a dollar. It fitted in my pocket. I had one bait, one rod and reel, one seat, and no back-up plan at all. Thank goodness I caught a fish on my second cast. Otherwise, my only other tactic was to pack up and go home. But at least these days when I go fishing I know what I'm trying to catch, and that's progress. The next step is obviously to introduce a set of alternative techniques that I can fall back on should my original tactics fail. I still don't like the sound of it.

THE BANKSIDE DETECTIVE

Choosing where to fish is partly about water craft (see Reading the Water on pages 82 and 83) and partly about common sense. It doesn't hurt to be a bit of a bankside detective, either.

Given that you may end up spending some time there, you should choose the spot where you're going to fish with care. The water next to those moored boats may look tempting when you arrive at 5 A.M. and everyone is asleep, but it's going to be transformed into a noisy, unfishable, up-and-down nightmare when things start moving. In the same way, those hoof prints leading to and from the water at the spot where you're planning to sit mean something, and if you set up at a spot where animals come down to the water, some will avoid you but others will try to walk through you and all your gear. Shame, because all those hooves in the water stir up the riverbed mud and attract the fish.

Think about the other factors as well, such as where the sun will rise and set, and which way the wind is blowing. Finally, check for signs like "Off-road motorbike contest here today."

PREVIOUS TENANTS

As a good bankside detective, look for the telltale signs that other anglers have been there before you: the remains of last night's fire, bait scattered carelessly near the water's edge, bits of line and other tackle trodden into the ground, the hole made by a rod rest, the grooves or other marks left by a fishing chair, and a pile of discarded cigarette butts. First, tidy up. I know you shouldn't have to, I know it drives you crazy, but it'll also give you karma points and, who knows, maybe even some luck.

Who's been fishing in my spot? A few minutes spent snooping around the bank can make all the difference.

If you notice only after studying the ground more carefully that other anglers have fished there recently, this can be a very good sign. Messy, careless anglers make a lot of noise, don't care about the fish or the environment, and are just as likely to throw rocks in the water — for fun, you know — after they've finished, rendering it useless for the next person. An angler who leaves little trace, on the other hand, may well have set things up nicely for anyone who follows by feeding bait into the spot carefully and quietly, and the fish may still be there and feeding.

I've certainly had some of my best sessions a few hours after a fishing competition, when the water has had a chance to calm down and the fish have moved back in to wolf all the bait that's been chucked in the water.

TACKLING UP AND PACKING UP

Many anglers can't wait to get to the water. You can see it in their faces, in the way they subconsciously accelerate the closer they get, the way — yes, it's true — their pupils dilate at the sight of a favorite stretch of water. And it's the same when it comes to packing up — they just chuck everything in the bag to sort out later. Tsk, tsk.

First, let me admit to some inconsistent behavior here, because on occasions I'm as bad as anyone. When the fishing frenzy is upon me, I'll dash lemming-like toward the water, destroying everything in my path, making a terrible racket, frightening fish for miles, slinging rod, reel, and end tackle together any-old-way and hoping that — like one of those collapsible tents — they'll all fall into place somehow.

It's nuts, of course. You should always take your time tackling up. It not only gives you a chance to get your gear straight, but it also lets you do the same

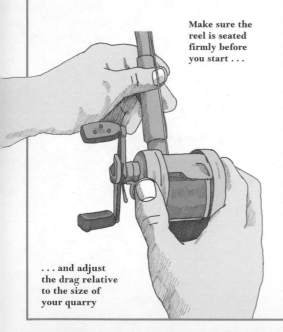

Make sure the reel is seated firmly before you start . . .

. . . and adjust the drag relative to the size of your quarry

thing for your head. This is a serious point. If you're anything like me, you will arrive at the lake or river carrying more baggage than just the stuff on your back, and tackling up gives you time to unload it.

SIMPLE CHECKS

While you're at it, do the simple things: check the end of your line to make sure there aren't any kinks in it from last time where you nipped off a weight or a stopper. Make sure your reel's running smoothly and that the drag's set up properly for whatever it is you're after — there's nothing worse than hooking a big fish that's right at the edge of what your tackle can handle, only to discover too late that it can't take line when it needs to because the drag is set too tight.

Once you let yourself relax into it, there's a wonderful rhythm to tackling up. Getting the rod out of its bag and putting it together. Folding the bag up and putting it away into the back pocket of your vest or your bag. Attaching the reel, snipping the end of the line off and wrapping the remnants round your fingers before putting them into a zip pocket so you can snip them and

Time spent setting up properly is always time well spent. At the very least, it gives you a chance to get your fishing head on.

throw them away when you get home. Threading the line through the eyes (and checking the eyes as you go), attaching the end tackle or the leader, preparing for the first cast. Watch someone who knows what they're doing and you'll notice how much it's about economy and precision, like a classical guitar player getting ready for a concert. Some anglers I know even flex their hands in the same way to loosen up.

TIME RUNS BACKWARD

Fast-forward to the end of a fishing session, and you should take the same kind of care when you're packing up your gear. With the exception of chess, fishing is the most absorbing of sports, so use the time spent packing up to unplug the part of your brain that does the fishing and re-engage the part that remembers where you parked the car and how to drive it. How well you pack up will be a function of how well you tackled up, because it most cases you're literally doing it in reverse; indeed, it sometimes feels as though you're in a film that's being rewound, or as if time itself was running backward. Of course, it goes without saying that, like any good citizen of the outdoors, you should treat nature's front room as if it were your own — so no litter, no dangerous bits of line, hooks, or other tackle left behind, thank you very much.

I remember trying to describe my love of angling to someone else and as I searched for a way to explain it I said: "I love everything about fishing. I even love packing up." It may be sad, but it's true.

No Fishing

I remember a river when I was a boy. To get there you had to cycle for about an hour and half, down one of the steepest hills you've ever seen (and consequently slog red-faced back up it on the way home), and then along the river valley.

For most of the valley floor the river was exposed and clearly on private land, but there was a stretch of about a mile where it meandered through thick woods and a determined boy could probably hide his bike in the bushes and wriggle through the fence. I didn't carry much in the way of tackle in those days (still don't), but it was still a struggle to get down to the water, especially at the end when I had to squeeze through almost on hands and knees.

The boy emerges from the bushes and peers at the thing in front of him, sticking out of the river. It's been waiting for him all long, ready to have the last laugh. He goes down on his haunches with a little harrumph. After a while he begins to brush the spiders from his hair.

GOOD LUCK

Ask any angler who knows anything about fishing, and they'll confess that the most important item in their tackle bag (apart, possibly, from that flask of coffee) is the company of Lady Luck. Expensive rods and reels, skill, a secret bait, the best spot on the lake . . . these are nothing in comparison to the importance of having Lady L on board, or maybe even in your pocket.

It's happened to me loads of times. I've sat in the fishiest-looking spot imaginable all day, peppering the water with free offerings, casting in the most succulent baits, the smelliest, fish-friendliest morsels on God's green earth, and caught nothing. Then, packing up, I've watched in disbelief as some noisy kid with a runny nose and a 30-year-old rod like a tree trunk settles into my spot and — first cast — hooks an absolute monster. Then, because they've got no proper gear, I always end up helping them to land it, take the hook out, weigh it, take their photograph, promise to send them a copy, and wade out into the lake to return the fish — at which point it does a merry flip out of my arms and crashes into the water, soaking me, while the kid falls about laughing. Once, before I quit, one lad even asked me for a smoke and sat in my chair afterward with a big grin on his spotty face, basking in that which he had and I lacked: luck.

THE KEY TO SUCCESS

You need to be lucky with the fish, the weather, where you choose to fish, which bait you use. In fact, all the things that you're supposed to be able to control through science, experience, and good techniques, you can just forget about. None of them are any good without luck. Athletes know this. It's why football players touch the grass and then kiss their fingers before they run onto the field; it's why they come out in a certain order or why they don't pull their shirts on until they're actually out on the turf.

How you get lucky is another matter. It's said that there are around 10,000 three-leaf clovers to every one with four leaves, so you can do the math on that one for yourself. While other tricks I've heard include throwing a pebble into the water before you start, dropping a coin into your fishing hole, wearing a silver (not gold) cross, and whistling against the wind.

Finally, *Guinness World Records* lists an 18-leaf clover as the record holder. It's said that the angler who found it is still playing the most enormous fish anyone has ever seen.

In case you can't find one of your own, feel free to use a copy of this four-leaf clover in emergencies.

ETIQUETTE

It may seem strange to talk of etiquette in the context of something so earthy, natural, and unmannered as angling, but it's an important part of the sport. If we don't consider the feelings of other anglers who share our passion, how are we to judge ourselves in the end?

You shouldn't need me to tell you that these floats are too close together. Keep your distance from other anglers, even when they're catching and you're not.

On the whole, we anglers are a fine bunch, quick to laugh and slow to anger — even in the face of overwhelming disaster (horizontal freezing rain, no bites all day, a procession of kids asking if you've "Had any luck yet?") we're more likely to ruffle the youngster's hair, smile wisely and say "Not yet, son" than growl and pour a tin of bait over his head. There is, however, an unwritten code that all good anglers follow, and these are the highlights.

Don't poach from someone else's spot, even if they're catching and you're not. It's impolite, bad form, and just plain desperate, too. Find your own fish. This issue has become more complex now that modern tackle allows almost any fool to cast the length of a football field with a flick of the wrist. This makes it possible to place your bait next to someone else's even when you're on opposite sides of the lake. Don't do it. If in doubt, put yourself in their shoes and you'll soon reel in. (I'm regularly overcast by anglers on the other side of one of my favorite rivers, but they're always apologetic, always reel in straight away and disappear down- or upstream with an embarrassed shake of the head. I like to think it's because I'm so silent, but it's usually because I've fallen asleep.)

IN THE MOOD FOR A CHAT?

Anglers generally enjoy a chat, but if the one you approach clearly doesn't, then leave them be. Similarly, it's important to read the body language of other anglers. If you come across one on his haunches, secreted behind a bush, inching his rod and bait out over the water, then there's probably a reason for it. He may not appreciate it if you come marching up, whistling and calling out "How's it going then? Any luck?"

It's acceptable to borrow the occasional item of tackle like a landing net or hemostats; it's reasonable to beg a smoke (but only one). If you're chatting and the coffee comes out, you may get a cup, but you should never ask. If you arrive at the same time as an another angler and it becomes clear that you're both heading for the same spot, you may be tempted to turn it into a race — don't. There's nothing quite so humiliating as two portly anglers, laden with gear, lolloping down the bank toward the same spot, like a pair of hippos lifting up their skirts and running.

TRADITIONAL BAITS

Despite the seemingly inevitable advance of science, there are still old-fashioned baits that anglers return to time and again. Sometimes it's because the bait in question reminds them of simpler times, and sometimes it's just a great bait that always does well. Here are some of the best.

For me it started with bread paste — sliced white bread, minus the crusts (the edges, really), mixed with cold tap water and kneaded until it made a sticky paste that could be wrapped in a handkerchief and carried safely in a pocket. Brown bread was no good because the fish didn't like it (neither did I, back then) and I used to think it was because they couldn't see it so well. I liked the idea of bread crumb, but couldn't get it to stay on the hook, and it always ended up sailing off into the air whenever I cast. Bread crust was reserved for carp anglers and was much too sophisticated for me.

Before my pocket money stretched to maggots, there were worms to be dug. My dad did gardening for a big house on the other side of the village, and he would let me come and raid the compost heap there for red wigglers with their funny little yellow rings and weird, pungent smell. I caught everything on those, including my first trout, out of a brook barely deep enough to cover its back. Fantastic bait, red worms.

Known in Britain as lobworms, and in the US as nightcrawlers, these big juicy wrigglers sure make a marvellous bait.

EXOTICA

Cheese paste was good too, especially for pumpkinseed. We discovered this exotic (back then) concoction when we ran out of bread paste and had to use half a cheese sandwich. Cheese spread was great as a variation, but only for still waters where you didn't have to cast very far, because it was too slippery to stay on the hook.

Nightcrawlers were brilliant for bass, walleye, and carp; hemp seed proved to be fantastically successful, once we'd realized you had to cook it first. Maggots stank but were always a winner, and on the first occasion that I arrived at the river to discover they'd turned into pupae, disappointment turned to joy when I discovered what a great bait they were — stink and all. I never did get the hang of using silkweed, though.

To this pantheon of traditional baits I'd add kernel corn in its old-fashioned non-chemically-enhanced form, straight out of the can. And, of course, luncheon meat — a classic fishing bait in the making, which has accounted for my biggest carp and has a growing reputation as a very effective and convenient catfish bait, yet remains, along with worms, the only bait I won't put in my mouth.

LEAVE NO TRACE

Amazingly, given their generally daft-as-a-brush characteristics, it was campers and hikers who came up with this idea — that people who use the outdoors should leave it as they found it, so that it's unspoiled for those who follow. Here in the US it's been elevated to a doctrine — but really it's just a fancy phrase for tidying up.

When you fish, remember that you're nature's guest and act accordingly.

Hardcore leave-no-tracers follow the code's seven principles, which are: plan ahead and prepare; travel and camp on durable surfaces; dispose of waste properly; leave what you find; minimize camp-fire impacts; respect wildlife; and be considerate to other visitors.

There's not really much to argue with there. Animal activists may hoot and holler at the idea that anglers respect wildlife, but good ones do, and the ones that don't are ignorant rather than evil. Anyway, all sensible anglers understand that pursuing the sport in a low-impact way is becoming increasingly important for fishing's survival.

TIDY UP

It's not as if being a good citizen of the outdoors is difficult. Take along a little plastic bag for all your rubbish, including the remains of lunch, soft-drink cans, bits of line, and the odd bit of tackle. Don't, don't, don't leave bits of line strewn around the bank, and if your gear gets caught in a tree make serious efforts to retrieve it, especially if there's still bait on the hook. When you get line home, snip it up into small lengths and trash it. Don't chuck stuff like empty cans and bottles in the water, either, because even if they sink they'll become very effective traps for small fish. If garbage cans are provided in a parking or picnic area, make sure you use them.

If you see someone dropping litter, it can be tricky. On the one hand you want to do the right thing; on the other, you don't want to get thumped. If there's the slightest chance of an argument, don't bother. Instead resign yourself to picking up after them when they've gone.

If the lake you use combines fishing and camping, then there'll probably be proper fire and barbecue sites you can use without creating your own. If not, then consider a camping stove to make hot drinks, or the marvellous Kelly kettle (see page 26).

If you need to create a way to the water where none exists, don't hack at it like an explorer. Do it sympathetically. This has the welcome side-effect of making it harder for other anglers to spot as well, so you may be able to keep it a secret for a little while longer.

HOW TO CAST

Golfers can talk endlessly about their swing — how unique it is, how hard it was to develop, how they've adapted it over the years to suit different conditions, clubs, and courses. How it's changed as they've grown older. Casting is the equivalent for anglers. We just don't go on about it all the time.

Well do I remember my early efforts at casting — the explosion as the tackle crashed into the water at my feet, or spun round and round in a tight, enormously dangerous circle in the air in front of me, or flew magnificently straight into the top branches of the tree on the opposite bank (or, even more embarrassingly, caught on the bush behind me).

Like many tricky things, the essence of casting is simple: you want to propel whatever is dangling from the end of your rod away from you so that it lands on a particular spot in the water. Watch someone who knows how to do it and be amazed at the way even an otherwise large and lumpy angler can be transformed into a thing of economy and grace.

The best way to practice casting is on your own, away from other people, and certainly nowhere near the water (I'm certain even the fish were laughing on my first day out). Since most people will be using a spinning reel (see page 11) we'll concentrate on that, though you'll find a bit of information about other kinds of reels on the following page.

HOW TO CAST

Set up your rod and reel and tie a small weight to the end to give you some casting momentum. Now you're ready for part one: releasing the line.

+ Hold the rod with the reel underneath.
+ Hold it in the hand you favour, leaving the other to wind the handle. Position your favored hand so that two fingers are in front of the reel stem and two are behind it; this allows you to hold the reel and rod loosely but securely.

Release the bail arm, hook your first finger over the line

Bring it forward smoothly and release the line

Swing the tackle gently back over your shoulder

Finish by pointing the rod where you want the bait to go

Other Kinds of Reel

Although most anglers use open-faced fixed-spool reels, there are other kinds you may come across.

+ Closed-face fixed spool: Same principle, but the face is covered by a cap which you push to release the line.
+ Spin-cast reel: Same principle, but it sits on top of the rod and has a catch at the back which you press to release the line.
+ Center-pin reel: An old-fashioned free-running round reel used mainly on rivers to fish with a float, a technique known as "trotting" the stream.
+ Baitcaster or multiplier reel: Like a science-fiction center-pin that sits on top of the rod and has a large line capacity, lots of gear power and is suitable for heavier lines of ten pound breaking strain or more; widely used in sea fishing.

A typical closed-face fixed-spool reel, mainly used for lure fishing.

+ Next, adjust the line length so that the weight is dangling about a foot (30 cm.) away from the end of the rod.
+ Hook your finger around the line in front of the bail arm and then release the arm.
+ Let go of the line and the weight will fall to the floor.

Now for part two: the swing.

+ Release line from the reel so that if you were to point the rod straight up in the air, your hook would hang one-third to one-half of the way down the rod.
+ Hook your finger around the line and open the bail arm.
+ Grip the end of the rod butt with your other hand and bring the rod back and over your head so that your favored forearm and hand are at 12 o'clock.
+ Sweep the rod forward and release the line from your finger when your forearm and hand are between 11 and 10 o'clock. Some anglers recommend that as you bring the rod forward you release the line at the moment you can point your index finger at the spot you're casting to. I think that's overly fussy, but see if it works for you.

And part three: different swings.

+ Some anglers hold the rod in front of them and bring it back absolutely straight as if they were holding a samurai sword.
+ Some naturally angle the rod toward their favored side by as much as 45°.
+ If you're casting a short distance or need to go under some overhanging trees, you'll need to perfect the underarm cast — here the trick is to hold the rod so your forearm and hand are at 10 o'clock and get the tackle swinging away from you and then toward you again like a pendulum.

Practice genuinely will make perfect (or close enough), but rarely will you see an angler who's mastered the art of casting so completely that they never screw it up. So relax and keep at it.

IN PRAISE OF THE KELLY KETTLE

Never underestimate the power of a hot drink on a cold, fishless day. Not only will it revive your spirits, it will also help to rekindle your cunning and send you back to the battle refreshed and reinvigorated.

A small stove of any kind is a good companion on the river bank. Fresh coffee, tea, or even hot chocolate, are great revivers at any time of the day. However, although any camping stove will suffice, when it comes to boiling water there's only one Kelly Kettle — a bizarre contraption based on a design that's more than 100 years old. Originally used by ghillies (servants who accompanied rich folk on hunting and fishing trips) in Ireland to make tea by the side of the loughs, the trick is in the kettle's unusual design, which features a hollow sleeve wrapped around a central top-to-bottom chimney.

INGENIOUS

To use it, take out the cork and fill the kettle with water. Position the separate base in such a way that the holes in the rim can pick up any breeze that's blowing, and start your fire in the base. Then put the kettle on to boil. Because the flames rise up and heat the whole of the inside of the chimney (as opposed to just the kettle bottom), the water boils much more quickly. To keep the fire going, just drop more fuel down the chimney. The kettle's not at all fussy and will burn with almost anything — sticks, twigs, and dried leaves and grass are all good. In winter, when everything's likely to be damp, I start the fire with a mini-firelighter and then add my special homemade fuel — strips of milk and orange-juice cartons folded accordian-style to burn longer and hotter.

When the water has boiled, you'll see steam coming out of the spout (never, ever boil your kettle with the cork still in it). Then you can lift the kettle carefully by the handle, take the cork in your other hand, and use it to tilt the kettle and pour the boiling water into cups. Save a bit of water to put out the fire in the base properly, and then scatter the ashes.

You have to take some fixings with you if you want use a kettle like this (coffee, milk, sugar and so on), but once you've made the effort the first time, it's unlikely you'll want to go back to an ordinary Thermos.

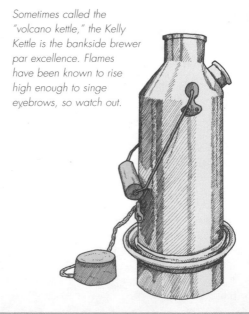

Sometimes called the "volcano kettle," the Kelly Kettle is the bankside brewer par excellence. Flames have been known to rise high enough to singe eyebrows, so watch out.

TIDDLERS

Despite what they may occasionally tell you or what you may read from time to time, all anglers will take a tiddler or two, if that's all that is available. Any angler who tells you otherwise is being economical with the you-know-what.

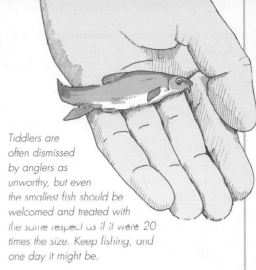

Tiddlers are often dismissed by anglers as unworthy, but even the smallest fish should be welcomed and treated with the same respect as if it were 20 times the size. Keep fishing, and one day it might be.

In your end is your beginning . . . or something like that. Certainly, when we begin our fishing lives, it's more likely to be in the company of small fish rather than large ones, and although as our careers progress we begin to believe we have the knack of catching what we like when we like, that golden period comes to an end all too quickly, dotage sets in and we're back where we started — clumsy, with slow reflexes, snagging the odd silver fish here and there.

I say this only because I've seen too many anglers treat too many small fish with disdain. In England, they call them names like "skimmers" or "shrapnel" or — even worse — "bits."

"Caught anything?"

"Just a few bits."

"Bits of what?" I always want to ask.

Tiddlers are defined differently by different people. To a small boy starting out, it's any silver fish that can be enclosed by the fingers of one hand; a few years later it's a salmon smolt that's seizes the fly intended for its grandfather; to the angler after large catfish or carp, it's a hungry five pound bass — a tiddler in every respect except actual size.

I'm always grateful for small fish, partly because sometimes it's all I can catch, and partly because it reminds me of the fish I caught all those years ago when I was starting out and when there was no need for a landing net because we never caught anything large enough to require one; and when it didn't matter what we caught, as long as it was something.

I've sat by my favorite summer stream, transformed by winter to a oily, sullen torrent, the color of cold tea. I've sat on the bank, teeth chattering, fumbling for the cigarettes I gave up long ago, looking wishfully at my watch, willing the hands round, trying to pull the sun out of the sky and chuck it over the horizon so the light would fail and I could just damn well go home. And then, when all hope has faded, the float has dipped or there's been a gentle tug on the rod and, miraculously, a small silver fish has appeared, sparkling from the freezing water, to tickle the palm of my hand and make — yet again — an angler's day. At times like that, size doesn't matter.

CASTING A FLY

Of all the styles of casting, fly fishing is the best. It's elegant, a supreme example of the angler's art, and it combines ribbon gymnastics, conducting, and lion taming into a single, fluid action to deliver something that weighs nothing. I don't know what all the fuss is about.

Like a golf swing, the art of casting a fly is a simple thing. You need to propel whatever is on the end of your line to a particular point in the water and have it land there naturally. The key word there is "naturally" — it must land in such a way that it attracts a fish rather than putting it down.

To make it more complicated — because fly anglers love making a simple thing complex almost as much as they love fishing — there are different kinds of fly casting depending on where you're fishing and what the conditions are like.

Remember that the central problem with fly fishing is that there's no weight on the end of the line, so you can't cast in the traditional sense. Instead, fly anglers use heavy main line with a very light length of end line to which they tie a fly. This means they have to use the weight of the line itself to make the cast, and this involves letting out line a little at a time, then casting it behind you, casting it forward, letting out more line, casting behind, bringing it forward and so on. This "false casting" is good for practising, but more than two or three will scare off a likely fish.

+ Start small. Find a clear area of grass, get set up as you would for fishing, but don't tie a hook on. Let about 20–25 feet (7–8 m.) of line out in front of you.
+ Stand nice and loose, pointing the rod out in front of you so the rod and line make a continuous straight line.

+ Hold the rod with your thumb resting on the top. During this whole process you're going to be moving your wrist and your forearm, NOT your shoulder.
+ Trap the line coming from the reel under a finger and raise the rod to 10 o'clock.
+ The first tricky bit. Flip the rod backward to pick the line up off the grass, and propel it behind you until the rod is at one o'clock.
+ Stop the movement sharply. Your wrist should be pointing straight up with the tip of the rod slightly behind you still at one o'clock.
+ Now the next really tricky bit. You have to pause and let the line straighten out behind you until you feel a gentle tug that means it's fully extended, at which point you . . .
+ . . . sweep forward and down, lowering your elbow as you go to help increase the acceleration. As your arm passes midday, snap the wrist to a stop to flick the line forward.
+ As the line sails over your head and onto the water (or where the water should be), lower the rod to follow it.
+ To increase the length of your cast you need to "shoot" the line. As the rod goes back, trap the line against the rod butt with a finger and pull a couple of yards of line off the reel with your other hand. As you bring the rod to its final forward position, release the line and it will "shoot" through the rod rings.

SOLUTIONS TO COMMON PROBLEMS

Easy as anything, right? Wrong. Even with plenty of practice, you'll find it takes time to master the fly cast. But that's OK because it keeps the riff-raff out. They've got no patience and aren't able to overcome common casting problems such as:

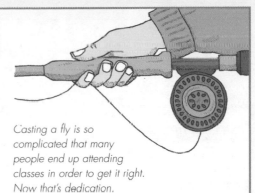

Casting a fly is so complicated that many people end up attending classes in order to get it right. Now that's dedication.

+ You'll be tempted to save time and jerk the line out of the water to begin the cast. Don't do this. It will disturb the water, put the fish down, and propel the line toward you at great speed. The rod needs to be lifted gently and smoothly at the beginning of a cast.

Here are the basics of the overhead fly cast, a thing of grace and beauty — once you've mastered it.

Begin to bring the rod up slowly . . .

. . . before flipping it backward behind you. Then, when you feel the tug . . .

. . . sweep the rod forward again, and as your arm passes midday, snap the wrist forward and release the line

+ Instead of going out behind you in a straight line, you may get a huge, baggy loop that eventually drapes itself unattractively around your ears. You need to stop the rod sharply without letting it go back too far. Imagine trying to cast the line straight up in the air instead of behind you.
+ There's an almighty crack (and, when fishing, the leader snaps off) when you bring the rod forward. This happens because you didn't pause long enough — wait for the tug — and you've erred toward the lion-taming end of things.
+ Instead of flying out straight in front of you, the line puddles in a heap in front of the rod — this happens because you didn't stop the rod firmly enough on the forward cast.

These are only a few of the most common problems you'll experience as a new fly caster, and they're presented here to give you an indication of the fun that lies ahead. And notice that we haven't even mentioned the roll cast or the double haul, the horseshoe or the steeple — let alone the dreaded double-handed Spey cast. For many anglers, fly casting is an endlessly fascinating obsession. Pick up a fly rod and prepare to join them.

WADING

There's nothing quite like getting into the water along with the fish. It changes your physical perspective, gets you closer to the water and to the fish, and it opens up all sorts of new spots you simply can't reach when you're fishing from the bank. It also makes you feel more connected to the fish and the fishing. Wading's amazing stuff.

First of all, make sure you're allowed to wade in the water. Sometimes you can't because it's considered too dangerous; other times it's because whoever owns the water rights has deemed that it disturbs the environment. It's your responsibility to find out how the land lies, rather than just wading in.

Assuming you can get in there, you need to get outfitted. Waders come in lots of different styles, but there are four main types: rubber, neoprene, and Gore-Tex*. Rubber is the least expensive and least comfortable; neoprene keeps you warm, while Gore-Tex offers the best of both worlds but is more expensive.

DIFFERENT STYLES
In terms of styles, rubber waders come with the boot built in and are available as chest waders as well as a lighter, thigh-length version for shallow streams. Neoprene and Gore-Tex chest waders usually end at the ankle so you have to buy separate boots. If you're concerned about falling in, choose neoprene waders for warmth and buoyancy.

When you're wading it's important to bear the following in mind:

+ Be cautious, and never try to wade and cast at the same time.
+ Try to stand side-on in fast current so as to offer less resistance to the water.

+ Always wear a wading belt and, in strong currents, a flotation device.
+ Never wade backward.
+ As you get older, think about using a staff to steady yourself.
+ In busy water, move one foot forward and then bring the other foot up behind it rather than walking normally — it's better for your balance.
+ Many anglers recommend you don't wade alone; crossing fast and difficult water is much easier if you're with a companion, because you can lock arms for extra stability.
+ When you cross a river, do so diagonally, moving downstream with the current as you go.
+ Remember you're wading for a purpose, not paddling around. The less you move, the less you'll spook the fish.
+ Always avoid large submerged boulders — they're extremely slippery.
+ If you're unlucky enough to fall in, try to get your knees up and maneuver yourself so that you're heading downstream feet first. That way you'll hit things with your feet rather than your head. Use your arms to try to get back to the shore.

* What happened to the fourth kind of wader? Bare legs and stout sandals! On a hot day, for short periods, there's nothing quite so refreshing.

IN THE DARK

Night fishing is all about preparation. That means you need to be familiar with the water — preferably the actual spot where you intend to fish — and you need to be organized enough so that you're not scrabbling around in the dark. I often try to keep everything I need in my pockets so that I don't have to get up and rummage around to find things — makes less noise, too.

Arrive before dark and get set up so that you know where everything is. In a perfect set-up, you shouldn't actually have to move from your seat to get what you need whether it's bait, tackle or — praise be — the landing net. Make sure that any bait is in a proper container. Assuming you're quiet enough, wild animals are surprisingly confident in the dark and will quite happily try to munch your bait if you let them.

Remember that a spot that's good to fish during the day may not be as good at night. Steep banks, trees, bushes, and other bankside growth that help to conceal the crafty angler in daylight simply become props for comedy pratfalls at night. You want a nice open spot with perhaps a friendly bush to hide behind, but not much more.

These glow-in-the-dark tubes contain two non-toxic chemicals separated by glass. Bending the tube cracks the glass, and the chemicals mix to produce a glowing light that lasts for up to six hours.

FISHING GEAR

If you're fishing a static bait, some kind of bite alarm is a good idea — I recommend that you make Ray's Bite Alarm (see page 92), which is simple, inexpensive, and doesn't disturb a peaceful night with some awful electronic buzzing.

If you're fishing with a float or ledgering with a soft-tipped rod, you'll need a glow-stick and something to attach it with. These neat little tubes come individually wrapped — crack one in half to produce a chemical glow that lasts for hours and is bright enough to see at a distance. Each one comes with either a small adaptor that fits on the rod or the float, or a strip of clear sticky tape to attach it. Anglers fishing from boats often lower a waterproof light and fish using that — after a while it actually attracts small fish, which in turn attract bigger ones.

LIGHTS

Take several lights. I always have a key-ring-style flashlight hanging off my vest in case I forget to bring a proper one. Headlamps are best because they leave your hands free. Lanterns lend a cozy glow to an evening, but they attract insects like crazy. Avoid waving your flashlight around the place — the point is to blend in, not draw attention to yourself.

FIVE FISHERMAN'S KNOTS

An angler's set-up is only as strong as its weakest link. Assuming you buy decent gear and look after it properly, this is likely to be either your line or the knots you tie in it. On these pages, you'll find step-by-step instructions on how to tie some key fishing knots that will serve a variety of purposes.

There are simply gazillions of fishing knots, with dozens of variations on the same theme and many different names. All I've done here is present the five that I use most often.

A couple of points. I'm actually something of a fan of hook tyers and have used them very successfully with eyed hooks. Simply follow the instructions that come with the hook tyer as if you were tying on a spade-end hook, but instead use a standard-eyed hook. The result is a great knot that's both small and strong.

Finally, although some people like to add a little daub of Super Glue to a knot, I prefer good old-fashioned spit. Simply wet the knot with your own saliva before tightening it, and it'll hold even better.

Mahseer knot

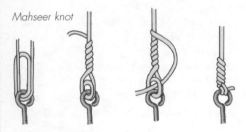

MAHSEER KNOT

For years I used a four-and-a-half-turn blood knot, which served me well — and still does for light lines and small hooks. For something bigger, however, I prefer the Mahseer knot. Here goes:

✦ Take the end of the line through the eye of the hook.

✦ Take it back on itself and thread it through again.

✦ Leaving a loop in place around the eye of the hook, wrap the end around the main line five times.

✦ Thread the end through the double loop and then, holding on to the end, slowly pull the knot tight. Trim the ends with line clippers.

✦ The blood knot is exactly the same, by the way, except you only thread the eye of the hook once.

PALOMAR KNOT

This is an alternative to the Mahseer knot and is useful for hooks, swivels, and so on. Some anglers rate it above the Mahseer, and after the initial threading, it's certainly easier to tie.

✦ Double up the end of the line to make a loop and thread this through the eye of the hook.

✦ Pull a fair bit through and then tie a simple overhand knot in the looped line so the hook dangles there.

✦ Pass the end of the loop over the point of the hook.

✦ Holding both ends of line, pull gently on the hook to tighten the knot, then trim the end.

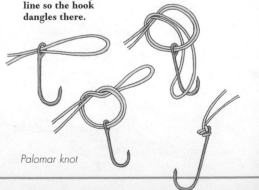

Palomar knot

HAIR RIG KNOT

This is designed for when you don't want the hook to go into the bait itself, but to hang next to it so that shy biting or suspicious fish are fooled into thinking that all is well.

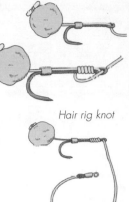

Hair rig knot

+ Take a short length of line and make a loop at one end.
+ Tie a simple over and under knot, leaving the small loop free.
+ Pull the loop through the bait using a boilie needle (a slim needle with a hook

on it) and then slip a stop into the loop and pull tight. You should now be able to dangle the bait on the line without it coming off.
+ Next, take the other end of the length of line and thread it through a bit of silicone tube.

Thread that onto the hook and take the end of the line through the hook eye.
+ Bring the line back and wind it round the shank five times.
+ Thread the line back through the hook and tie on a swivel with a Mahseer or Palomar knot as described on the previous page.

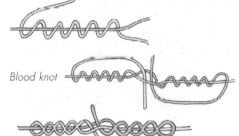

Blood knot

BLOOD KNOT

There are a number of variations on this knot, which is useful for tying two lengths of line together directly without using a swivel. The one shown here is the easiest version.

+ Make sure the two lengths of line overlap each other.
+ Take one end of the line and wrap it five times round the other piece.
+ Bring the end back and pass it between the two lines.
+ Repeat with the other line so it turns

five times and then comes back through the opening in the middle.
+ Holding the free ends of both pieces of line, gently pull first one length of line and then the other, working the knot so that it tightens.
+ Trim the ends off.

FLOAT STOP KNOT

If you want a free-running float (to fish at depth, for example), you'll find it useful to have a stop knot to prevent it from going too far up the line. Never attempt to tie a knot in the main line itself. Instead, use this.

+ Snip a short length of line from the main line.
+ Locate the position on the main line where you want to have the stop knot, then turn the short piece of line around it three times.

+ Take the two free ends of the short piece of line and make a double overhand knot.
+ Tighten the knot and snip the ends off.

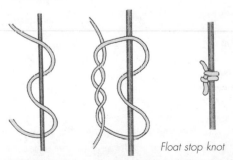

Float stop knot

FISHING FRIENDS

Although I've argued elsewhere that angling is essentially a solitary sport, if you can find a good fishing friend whose rhythms match yours, who's happy to car-share, to meet on the bank for the occasional smoke or hot drink or chat but will otherwise leave you in peace, then hang on to them. Such people are hard to find and should be cherished.

I've been fortunate enough to have made some good angling friends over the years. The bar was first set by my friend Keith, who was the son of a local policeman and whose Mom could rustle up gut-busting breakfasts at the drop of a landing net. Keith's nickname was "Bount" and mine was "Beat," and we discovered fishing together, first with nets and later with rod and reel.

In between, Bount announced that he intended everyone — including his family — to start calling him "Chick," and although it was never clear to me why he wanted to break up the Bount and Beat routine, I was happy enough to oblige. Anyway, he had access to something special — a small pond hidden in some woods that a local landowner had decreed was only for use by emergency services — fire, police, and ambulance. Since Chick's dad was a fully paid-up police officer, we were in.

ISLAND LIFE

And what a place it was. It had an island in the middle, steep banks, and it had fish — big fish, like bass and carp, that we'd never seen before. Of course, it had a monster pike ("Oooh look, Chick, it's got another labrador.") and plenty of small perch and rudd. And of course, that fabulous, fateful island. Since Chick was the only one of us who could afford waders, it was decided that he would wade across to the island

A little too close for comfort? Not if you respect each other's space and understand when it's time for talk and when it's time for silence.

carrying the gear before coming back for me. The first part went exactly according to plan, but halfway over with me on his back, Chick listed suddenly to one side. As he tried to right himself his boot sank further into the mud, and just before he fell over completely I did what any true friend would do in the same situation — I wriggled free from his grip, and as he fell forward, placed my foot firmly on his back for purchase and kicked off for the shore. Now, as Newton tells us, for every action there is an equal and opposite reaction, and as I landed safe (and dry) upon the shore, Chick fell face-down in the muddy water. If it hadn't been for the fact that I was now the only one with any dry smokes, I think I would still be on the island to this day.

STRESS-BUSTING

Fast forward 20 years. Apart from the odd half-hearted trip, I've barely fished at all — side-tracked by university, a growing interest in drama, that girl, all the usual stuff that takes you over in your 20s and 30s — but I've still got a few bits of gear hanging about, so when Ray suggests fishing as a possible antidote to all the stress I'm getting at work, I figure that anything's worth a try. It's winter, of course, and as we bundle into Ray's car — along with his brother Alex and some German guy — I feel my chances are slim. They get even slimmer when we arrive at the water and I discover that I don't have a reel. Fortunately, Ray has a spare, but it makes me feel like a dork and, true to form, I don't catch anything. Don't even get a bite.

Another year passes, things don't get any easier at work, and once again Ray suggests fishing. Again it's the dead of winter, dark by 4.15 P.M., freezing cold and fishless, but for a few wonderful moments I make contact with a small carp and, even though it gets off, I'm still thinking about it as I pack up. Later, watching the first stars through the branches of bare trees, I listen to Ray putting his gear away and suddenly everything slips into place. Fishing friends are there for you. They carry you on their backs. They help you find the magic again.

The Hat

Of all the various items of attire that an angler comes to love, none is quite so close to the heart as a good hat. It's not just about keeping the rain off or shading you from the sun. It's more how it feels when you put it on, how it becomes part of the ritual of preparing to fish. My hat is always the last thing on, and I make sure that I take it off again when I get back in the car. Currently it's a baseball cap with the words "Fairport Convention" on it — they're a folk-rock band who've been together for 40 years, and anything that's associated with that least-fashionable genre of music must have some luck attached to it. Often that's what the choice of a good hat comes down to — a bit of luck, a bit of superstition.

If you're buying a new one (all hats fall apart eventually), you need a large waterproof brim that can protrude from a hood to keep you dry and stop the sun from blinding you when it's hot. You may want something that has flaps that come down and cover your ears in winter, bloodhound-style (I do), but that's it. Everything else is either personal taste or a luxury.

🐟 THE WATER NOT FISHED

Although anglers always remember the lakes and rivers where they've been lucky enough to while away a few happy hours, there are always other waters that for one reason or another they've never been able to fish. You can't help but wonder what might have been.

It started when I was a boy in England, reading about places that existed only in the pages of books. Top of the list was Redmire Pool, secret home to giant carp, but there were also the Rivers Derwent and Swale in Yorkshire, Billing Aquadrome in Northants where enterprising anglers were catching huge carp on bananas, Hickling Broad in Norfolk where rudd the size of dinner plates were commonplace, and the famous milk-pool swim on the Fairy Water in Omagh, Northern Ireland — though what it was famous for I never did find out. These were vivid waters, whose remote banks I would never tread.

Others were closer geographically but just as distant in terms of access, glimpsed from the window of my dad's car or rocking back and forth on the occasional train journey, nose pressed against the window. A bicycle opened some doors, but it was the bus that first took me past the great Thames and it was on trains that I discovered what a wealth of water was available to the adventurous angler, most of which remains unfished by me and, I suspect, by most of us.

FINDING NEW WATERS

I used to find the thought of all that water without me next to it downright depressing, but now it excites the hell out of me and I can sit for hours with a proper topological map, looking for little pools of blue nestling in hills or hidden away deep in woods. I've found lovely

On long journeys I'd gaze longingly out of the window at all that water — trainspotting took on a whole new meaning . . .

private ponds like this where the farmer is usually happy to let you fish now and again (although I've also been sent packing on more than one occasion.)

And now, with the arrival of computer programs like Google Earth, it's possible to extend the fantasy still further and visit Lake Baikal in Siberia or the rocky streams of Vancouver Island, if only virtually. I can follow my friend Ian on his trip to Mongolia to catch taimen, watch Sean clambering over the rocks on the Hurunui in New Zealand, and I can finally visit Redmire Pool and imagine myself leaning on the old wooden posts overlooking the dam . . . if only someone would tell me where it was.

WILDLIFE

As we'll see elsewhere in the book, there are lots of other water users that anglers need to rub along with, but none are more important or rewarding than the animals who have made it their homes. Whether the fellow creatures in your neck of the woods include eagles or robins, rabbits or rattlers, it's a point worth remembering: we're just visiting — they live here.

Apart from bird watchers, I can't think of another countryside visitor who will come here and then sit quietly for hours on end, sinking into the landscape until they become almost a part of it (I don't include hunters, because they periodically destroy the illusion of peace with all those bangs). This stillness gives anglers a unique perspective, a privileged peek through Nature's back door.

Sometimes the animals are enough to turn a poor fishing day into a fine one. Even if you've not had a bite all day, you've kicked your bait into the water and snapped your landing-net handle by sitting on it, you can't fail to be moved by a kingfisher zipping down the river, inches from the surface, a personal parade of color on a cold, cheerless day.

They may not be wild, but I find cows a great tonic, too, because they're so big and dopey. This summer I had 13 of them follow me up and down the field all day, thinking they were going to be fed or milked . . . or maybe they just wanted a chat. They were easy enough to lose by ducking behind a bush, crossing a foot-bridge, or jumping a fence, but after a while I missed them and so I wandered back into the field to carry on fishing, whereupon they gently stampeded across the meadow to start the game all over again.

I've seen deer, snakes, mink, otters, and, late one summer's evening, a large gray owl going about its business, quartering the fields by the river, searching for shrews, voles, and rabbits. They don't make a sound when they fly, which is amazing for a bird so big. No more sound than the hot-air balloons that are regular visitors in the summer months, floating in the high air.

Sometimes, when the fishing is slow or I've stopped for a cup of tea, I wonder what the scene looks like from up there, and whether I fit in with the rest of the wildlife as much as I'd like to, or if, despite our best intentions, anglers still stick out like so many sore thumbs.

Where would the bored angler be without cows for entertainment? I mean, look at them watching you watching them.

🐟 MONSTERS

Every angler has a monster in their life that haunts them in ways more disturbing than any Stephen King-concocted creature can ever hope to match. Mind you, there's one similarity between anglers and King's characters — we both seek out the monster, one way or another.

There's no real definition of a monster, but I think it's a fish that's glimpsed, seen out of the corner of your eye, maybe deduced from a faded record of stocked fish, or perhaps the subject of a conversation overheard in a bar. In short, I don't think it's a fish that you can ever catch.

My first monster was a golden trout in the local pond, said to occupy a hard-to-get-to spot round the side where the big houses backed onto the water, but where a small boy could inch his way round without attracting attention if he was quiet enough. I rarely was. The one occasion I made it round without

The thing about monsters is that they're always there, just beneath the surface, ready to show their true selves at any moment. Anglers need monsters and always will.

getting chucked off, I swear I saw it move just under the surface with a sort of Fort Knox flash, and I ran back to tell my friends. It was a lie, of course. I never saw a thing, while my float sat unmoving in a tiny patch of oily water between the lilies.

I didn't care about the lie, though, and I still don't, because it was for the greater good. The myth of the monster golden trout was preserved, and that night, the dreams of small boys were golden, full of dipping bobbers and bent rods.

Down the years came other monsters. There was the giant pike, large as a log, that hung around like a gangster in the corner of an ancient pond, ready to do violence, and the monster salmon in the south-west of England that, if I'm honest, turned out to be an actual log. There was a monster the length of my forearm in a clear southern chalk stream, grown huge from table scraps, and one summer evening on a tiny Sussex river, something enormous that tore off with my nightcrawler as if behind the wheel of a car.

I never caught any of these fish and I'm not sure that I'd ever want to (apart from that roach — I mean, what a fish!), because the nature of all good monsters is to remain unseen until the final scene. And I'm not quite ready for the lights to go up just yet.

LINES

Often neglected, or skimped on by beginners, the kind of line you use and how you use it can make a significant difference to how successful you are as an angler. If only it wasn't such a boring subject . . .

It's what connects you to the fish, so choose your line with care. Look after it well and it'll repay you with good service.

Obviously there are many different brands of fishing line, and you should take advice from your tackle shop on which to get — depending on the thickness of your wallet. For what it's worth I've always found Maxima to be reasonably priced and reliable. Brands aside, there are two main types of line: monofilament, which most anglers use all the time, and braid, which is mainly used in special situations.

Monofilament lines are distinguished by breaking strain and color. I've never been a particular believer that color makes much difference, unless you're fishing incredibly clear water, so I usually opt for grays, browns, and greens. In terms of breaking strain, I go for the lightest I can without endangering the fish. This is crucial. It's all very well fishing so light that you get lots of bites, but it's no good if you keep losing fish to line breaks, and you should increase the breaking strain. Other determining factors should include the species you're after (bass fight harder than walleye), what the water conditions are like (weeds may be more troublesome in summer, the water may be clearer in winter), and whether you're fishing with a bobber or rolling the bait along the bottom.

Very broadly speaking, I fish lighter in winter when bites are harder to come by and the bottom is likely to be less snaggy. Float-fishing for small fish, I'd use 2–3 lb. line; ledgering for larger ones I'd go to 6 lb. In summer I'd fish 4–5 lb. on the float and 8 lb. upward on the ledger. For pike and carp I start at 10 lb. and go up to 15 lb. Just like a guitar string, fishing line needs to be changed from time to time, because no matter how well you treat it (and almost no-one treats line well), it loses its lustre, stretch, and strength. I replace my line every season without fail, and I can't remember the last time I lost a fish because the line snapped. To make your line to float, rub a little diluted washing-up liquid along it — this is helpful if you're float fishing.

Braid tends to have a narrower diameter than monofilament, is stronger, and doesn't stretch at all; it's also better if you're dragging or rolling a bait across the bottom, because it resists abrasion.

Finally, there's lots of talk about fancy new lines made of materials like fluorocarbon, which has the same refractive index as water and thus becomes invisible when submerged. However, I'm not a big fan because I've heard bad things about the manufacturing process and that it degrades incredibly slowly.

THE FIRST CAST

The first cast of the day is a deceptively simple movement. On the face of it, it's nothing more than mechanical, a means of getting the bait in the water and in front of the fish, but it can also be a thing of beauty. I've seen anglers casting with such economy and grace, it was as if they were painting in the air. The first cast is the beginning of so many things.

These days it's a longer walk to the river than before, or maybe as I get older it just feels that way. Since the residents decided no one else is allowed to park in the lane, we have to leave our cars up on the common and walk the rest of the way on foot. It's OK for me because I travel light — a single rod, landing net and one rod rest, creel slung over a shoulder with a reel inside along with a small tackle box, inflatable cushion for a seat, cloth, and small Thermos. If it's a longer trip, I'll take the Kelly Kettle, which hooks onto my waistcoat but is light enough not to notice. It's also nice on a winter's morning — it gets the blood moving and, after the long drive, gives my injured knee a chance to click through the gears until something like normal service is resumed.

It's early morning in November and there's been a sudden hard frost, which I'm hoping won't put the fish down. The cold snap has turned the common into something of real beauty, and at this time there's only me and the odd dog walker to spoil it.

HEAVY HORSES

Down the lane past a couple of houses I go. They're dark, but the one at the end on its own by the first gate has a downstairs light on. I can see into the kitchen where there's a fire being

The bait is finally in the water and the effect is amazing — a sense of complete calm combined with the kind of crackling in the air you get from being too near to an enormous generator.

started and there's a pot of coffee on to brew. It makes me think of Christmas. Through the gate I go, and over the field. Here there are usually horses, not high-stepping racers but not nags either, and if you don't make any sudden moves you can usually coax one or two to the fence and they'll nuzzle your pockets looking for apples. When I smoked I'd quite often stop here, roll a cigarette, and watch them for ten minutes (this apparent time-wasting is a hangover from one particular winter morning when I arrived so early that I couldn't see to tackle up and so had to wait by the river for the sun to rise).

Then it's through another gate and on to the spot where you can hear the roaring of the dam as the water pounds through the sluices. Standing on top of it, I admire the magnificent contrast — the placid canal-like stretch above the dam and the boiling water below it, gathering pace before hitting the shallows at the bend and bubbling onward.

I'm nearly there now. The canal is on my left, squared away and tidy, perhaps a foretaste of what awaits all rivers, but for now on my right I can hear the faint sound of the real thing through the trees and, with excitement building, I carefully make my way through the thickets toward a likely spot, clambering over a fallen oak, unshipping my gear, and surveying the water hopefully.

It's damn near perfect. Fast water in the middle, lots of interesting slacks nearer to my bank, an eddy on the far side, strange currents whirling where the two meet. There are trees, too, overhanging the far bank, which make for a difficult cast, but if you get it right you can roll a bait under them and who knows what might be waiting?

Elegant Casting

I'm not sure I can remember my first cast. It wouldn't have been very elegant, that's for sure, because back then I was under the impression that better anglers used heavier line (because they were better at fishing, they were more likely to catch larger fish, and thus needed stronger line). I remember using line with a 14 lb. breaking strain, which was devilishly difficult to thread through the eye of a size 16 hook. I've said it before and I'll say it again — I deserved every one of those pan fish.

PREPARATORY MATTERS

I set up the landing net and throw in a few handfuls of loose feed, mainly chunks of luncheon meat that I've torn into small pieces to let the oils and scent escape more easily. Then I tackle up, keeping things as simple as possible — 8 lb. line straight through to a size 6 hook, large piece of meat for bait, no end tackle at all. I inflate a small camping pillow — red side facing me, blue side facing the water, an old superstition — and pop it on the ground. I ease onto the pillow. The rod rest goes in, the cloth comes out beside me, the bait on top of that. I adjust my hat and make sure my hemostats are hanging from the front of my vest. There's nothing left to do. I take the bail arm off, swing the bait out over the water and watch fascinated as it sails under the tree and lands in the water, with what I hope is a fish-enticing splosh.

And there I sit. The boy, still fishing.

HOW TO STRIKE

Of all the skills that the newcomer to fishing must master, the one that seems most like one of the black arts is the successful strike. On the face of it, you'd think there was plenty of cause and effect to be going on with, because a strike is simply the movement of the rod in response to the bite that sets the hook. The thigh bone's connected to the hip bone, and all that.

First, a little secret. Although it feels as though Newton's third law of motion (for every action there is an equal and opposite reaction) ought to make its presence felt here, there's a lot more to a good strike than simple cause and effect. Sorry about that. For a start, there are just too many variables involved — whether you're fishing still or running water, whether it's summer or winter, whether you're using monofilament or braid (mono "gives" while braid does not), hook size, how your float is set up, how big the weight on the end tackle is, whether you're fishing a lure, or a fly, or a different kind of fly, whether the place is heavily fished or not and the bites are shy, how big the fish is, how big the bait is, the size of the fish's mouth, the size of your hook … you get the idea.

What we can do, though, is paint with the broadest of brush strokes in order to get you started. With that in mind, here are the can't-miss-'em strikes:

✦ If you're lure-fishing (and that includes dead-baiting), most of the time you can get away with doing nothing because the fish will hook itself when it slams into the lure. Easy. Strike one for us.
✦ If you're fishing for anything that picks up a bait and runs (or perhaps that should be swims) with it, then

simply lifting the rod and hanging on is enough. Strike two.
✦ Similarly, aggressive fish that like large baits will often hook themselves. All you have to do is grab the rod to stop it from being pulled in. Strike three.
✦ Certain rigs are designed so that the fish hook themselves. Strike four. This is easy, no?

Naturally, not all fish are so obliging, and I've also sat in the same spot using the same tactics and felt a carp plucking at the bait with its barbules as if playing the most delicate of harp strings, and certainly offering nothing definite enough to strike. So, at the risk of laying myself open to outright ridicule, here are my rules for striking:

✦ If you're float-fishing for tiddlers, strike fast and hard when the float goes under, using an action as if you were pulling your hand out of a savage dog's mouth.
✦ Do a slower variation of the same movement if the float sidles away without going under, especially if it's on a river and against the current. Imagine the dog is still there, but not quite as savage.
✦ If you're after larger fish on the float, give them time to actually make off with the bait — this will

usually involve the float disappearing under the water and moving off with purpose. When this happens, lift the rod with a slower, smoother action as if the end you're holding was the root of a cow's tail, flicking gently at flies.

+ If you're bottom fishing and get a good solid pull, simply pulling back will be enough to set the hook.
+ If you're getting little tugs and plucks, it could be small fish picking over the bait or a large fish coming over all shy and sensitive. Try striking sharply at some of these and see what happens.
+ Alternatively, point the rod at the bait, pull a little bit of line off the reel, and feel for bites with your fingers. This is called "touch ledgering" and is good for picking up the most delicate bites.

The best advice is to be patient with yourself and to understand that — like most things connected with angling — striking is an inexact science that requires practice. Fortunately, adopting this attitude gives you the perfect excuse to go fishing again.

The strike having been successfully negotiated, the joyful angler can play the fish toward the bank — unless he messes it up.

Art, Sport, or Science?

Samuel Johnson wrote: " . . . angling or float fishing I can only compare to a stick and a string, with a worm at one end and a fool at the other." Which only goes to show he should have stuck to literary criticism.

Of all the pursuits that sensible folk take up, angling is arguably the hardest to pin down. Some hobbies are easy. Hockey is merely a sport ("The coolest game on Earth," or not). So is pool or even golf. Cookery, on the other hand, combines science and chance with a decent end product. Gardening is science, provides physical exercise, and, even if you only plant flower beds, has a dash of art. Chess is a sport and a science, while drinking is simply a pastime — whatever your friends tell you.

Angling, on the other hand, is art, science, and sport combined into such a rich and heady brew that it's no wonder we are consumed.

See the patterns a fly caster paints in the air; look at the crafty angler at work in the kitchen, mixing the ingredients to create a new super-bait; watch the fight with a 10 lb. fish from start to finish; and then tell me this isn't the most extraordinary pursuit ever invented by the wit of humankind.

UNLIKELY BAITS

You don't like to eat the same food every day, and neither do the fish. So why not give them a treat — and yourself a laugh — by trying out some of these bizarre baits?

As the diet enjoyed by a typical fish becomes richer, more varied, and easier to come by, it stands to reason that, like people, fish are going to prefer to eat the things that they enjoy the most. Now "enjoy" is probably getting a bit anthropomorphic in these circumstances, so let's broaden it to mean plentiful, easy to swallow, strong-smelling, and maybe even unusual. I'm not saying you can sling any old thing on the hook and expect a bite (though God knows, anglers have caught fish on some pretty strange "bait"), but if you persevere by introducing the substance slowly over time, you can get a fish to feed on almost anything. For example:

Dried pet foods such as dog and cat biscuits are extremely successful baits when soaked in a little hot water.

+ Dried pet food. Seriously: pop some dried dog biscuits in a plastic bag, pour in a little hot water, give it a good shake to coat them all, twist it shut to seal the bag, and go fishing. By the time you get where you're going, they'll be soft enough to go on the hook but firm enough so they don't fly off when you cast. They float, too, so you can free-line them for fish that feed on the surface, or fish them with a weight on the bottom so they pop up and wave attractively in the current.

+ Raw steak. Yes, I know that some people think this is a waste, but most fish are carnivorous and enjoy the occasional mouthful of raw meat. Fortunately, it doesn't have to be a very good cut!

+ Fish food. Not the silly flakes you feed to goldfish, but the brown, smelly pellets that are fed to farmed trout and salmon. You can mix them with water to form a foul-smelling paste that's loved by all sorts of different fish. Of course, nobody will want to shake hands with you ever again.

+ Potato peelings, tin foil, soap, red wool, flowers, liquorice, rabbit droppings . . . in fact, there's a school of thought that says if you can get it to stay on a hook, then it's fish bait, and something out there will wolf it down.

Out on a Limb

The moral of the story is that anglers need to be prepared to try everything in the search for success. Improvization is a useful skill. If you arrive at the bank only to discover that all your bait is still in the fridge back home, you may be able to find alternatives — and successful ones at that — where you least expect them.

THE SECRET LAKE

Every angler has one of these, or dreams of having one. It's the lake that no one else knows about or that hasn't been fished for years. It's the tiny pond that has lost its memory and lies unconsidered in a wood.

Myths accumulate round these places, and over time their status grows to legendary proportions. It's a chance conversation overheard in the bar, the stranger you meet at the bus stop who has a faraway smile on his face and, having taken the third nip from a hip flask, lets his guard down long enough to pass on a tantalizing hint or two. It's the flash of water glimpsed from the window of a train at dusk, a tiny irregular blue symbol on a map, miles from anywhere.

It's rarely a river, because rivers cover more ground and are harder to conceal. It's often a pond, because ponds are small and easier to hide. You know when you've found one as well. It's hard to get to the water's edge and it doesn't have that "tidied away" look about it — there are certainly no obvious places to fish. Best of all, there are none of the subtle signs that the spot is frequented by people — no cigarette butts, no wrappers, no empty beer cans or bits of line trodden carelessly into the ground. So you must fish with care and keep your silence; and when you leave, let the secret lake sink back into the landscape again until the next time.

CARING FOR YOUR RODS

The beauty of modern carbon-fiber rods (or even older fiberglass ones) is that they need barely any care and maintenance at all.

In fact, unless you've paid out a lot of money for a specialist rod and want to lavish a bit of attention on it, I'd recommend you leave your rods well alone. Cork handles will change color as a result of age, water and the oil from an angler's hands, but it's just part of the natural aging process and you can leave them be.

I never bother to dry my rods unless I've done a bit of sea fishing, in which case I'll sluice them down with a watering can of rainwater from the barrel and dry them off with the rod bag — just to get rid of the salt.

I check rod rings regularly for signs of wear and tear, because nothing abrades line like a ring guide that's become pitted. Just pull a cotton ball through the ring and see if any gets left behind.

If a rod becomes hard to put together and take apart, rub a little candle wax on the male ferrule. Cane rods are different in this respect (see page 102). But the most important part of rod care is transporting it properly — take particular care when you're carrying it or getting it in and out of the car. Revolving doors are the worst. I remember one time . . .

LURE FISHING

One of the most exciting branches of angling, lure fishing can account for some huge fish. It keeps you on the move, works all year round, and can bring results when the more sedate forms of predator fishing are proving fruitless. (Note to self: must do more lure fishing.)

Although lures can be large or small, long or short, hard or soft, real or man-made, they're all trying to do the same job — that is, fool the fish into thinking that they're something good to eat. The design of the lure helps with this, but it's also up to the angler to retrieve the lure in the correct way in order to attract a passing predator.

Big fish that eat little fish aren't concerned about being sporting. If they can grab an easy meal courtesy of a dead or dying fish, then that's what they'll do — staying at the top of the food chain is all about acquiring the most calories while expending the least amount of energy. Pleasure anglers know this, if only because of the number of times in a fishing year that they bring a small fish to the net only to have it snaffled (just when it looks at its most helpless) by a passing predator.

There are a number of different factors that determine whether or not a predator is attracted to a lure, and it's not at all clear whether it's possible to rate them in

This classic spoon style flashes and vibrates like a small fish in trouble to attract predators.

any kind of meaningful order. Certainly vibrations are very important and are used by fish to locate food. We also know that they're able to see some colors at depth and distance more clearly than others. The behavior of the lure counts as well — a straight, overly fast retrieve isn't going to be as attractive as a variable one that makes it look as though the lure is in trouble or sick.

Of course, this being angling, there are enough different types of lure to decorate a Christmas tree (or at least fill the shelves of a tackle dealer), but as always, how you use a lure counts at least as much as what kind you buy. Let's have a look at the most useful ones.

OLD-FASHIONED SPOONS AND SPINNERS
These are designed to either wobble or spin through the water, sending out vibrations to nearby predators and flashing in the water the way the scales on a real fish would. Some spoons are too heavy to fish comfortably in shallow water because you have to retrieve them so quickly that they don't look at all like real fish.

Plugs come in all shapes and sizes. Some are designed to dive, while others are designed to wobble across the surface.

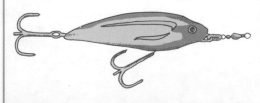

PLUGS

There are lots of different kinds of these, mostly made of plastic (but sometimes metal or wood), and they're designed to mimic the way prey fish move through the water. Some anglers like to make or at least decorate their own plugs in the belief that they can improve on shop-bought ones. These are the main types:

+ Floating–diving plugs. These float until you start to retrieve them, at which point the vane at the front makes them dive. The faster you wind in, the deeper they go.
+ Floating plugs. These stay on the surface during the retrieve and mimic all kinds of little mammals and amphibians that fish like to eat. Varying the retrieve causes them to flap about, which attracts predators.
+ Diving plugs. These stay under the surface all the time and are most useful if you're fishing very deep water. Let the plug hit the surface, count a set number of seconds to let it sink, and then start to retrieve. Altering the count changes the depth at which the lure is being fished.
+ Suspended plugs. These are peculiar things — when you retrieve, they dive; when you stop, they neither sink nor float but just sort of sit there, waiting for you to start the retrieve again.

The fact that no one's ever seen a fish like this won't necessarily stop it from attracting the interest of a hungry — and stupid — predator.

Handle with Care

Despite their ferocity, predators need careful handling when you get them to the bank, where their size and natural aggression can provoke inexperienced anglers to treat them roughly. They need the same consideration as any other fish — an unhooking mat or other soft surface, wet hands, a wet cloth — but in addition you may also need long-handled hemostats, side cutters to snip through difficult-to-remove hooks, and some small pliers.

If you're at all uncertain, go with a more experienced friend a few times until you feel more confident. There are few things more satisfying than fighting a fish to a standstill and then unhooking it successfully, letting it recover and then watching it swim off, as strong as ever.

RUBBER JIGS

These are the prosthetics of the lure-fishing world, made from rubber that can be fashioned into almost anything — worms, crayfish, frogs, prawns, sand eels, you can pretty much name it — and are wound back in by working the rod up and down and slowing down or speeding up the retrieve. To my mind, one of the advantages of rubber jigs is that many of them come with a single hook rather than the double or treble hooks favored in many other types of lure designs. This makes them much easier to remove from a fish's mouth.

HOW TO PLAY — AND LAND — A FISH

Of all the different steps that are required before you can catch a fish, none is as satisfying as the fight itself. The feel of a living, breathing creature on the end of your line, where moments ago there was nothing, is deep and resonating.

SMALL FISH

Small fish are easy to land and don't really require any playing at all because they're very small. If they're tiddlers, take care not to damage their mouths by bringing them in too fast. If you're fishing with kids, discourage them from artificially extending the "fight" by leaving the fish in the water too long and playing with it the way a cat plays with a mouse; it'll tire the fish to exhaustion and is a good way to get it attacked by a passing predator, which will be attracted by the fish's gradually weakening movements. Anything up to the size of an adult hand can be swung to shore, rather than brought in with a landing net. Never chuck any kind of fish back into the water — you don't want to give them a concussion.

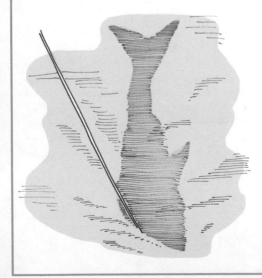

MEDIUM-SIZED FISH

I'm going to class medium as anything up to 3 lb., regardless of species. This is going to give you more of a fight, and you'll need to keep constant tension on the line from the moment you strike until you land the fish with the net (if you get snagged, check out some of the strategies on page 71). Unless you're fishing with very light tackle, your superior strength, the elasticity of your line, and the power of your rod and reel will make this a pretty one-sided — though still enjoyable — affair, and you'll be surprised at the tenacity and strength of some species.

LARGE FISH

I reckon that anything between 3 lb. and 10 lb. is a large fish. It isn't if you go fishing for carp or pike every week, but for most pleasure anglers, a fish of 10 lb. is a big event in the fishing year, and some of us won't see too many of them. Now you're getting into some serious fighting territory and you can expect not just solid tension on the rod, but also that the fish will take some line from your reel. This is OK, since you remembered to set the drag up correctly so the fish can take line in a controlled fashion before it breaks. If a fish can take line too easily, you'll be forever winding in while the fish continues to take line, and neither of you will get anywhere.

The moment when you bring a fish to the surface and can identify it is one of the most exciting parts of the fight.

It's important to keep the pressure up on larger fish, especially if you're using a barbless hook.

SPECIMEN FISH

Here we're in 10 lb.-and-above territory and pretty much anything can happen. It's quite likely that the fish on the other end weighs more (or is capable of generating more weight if you let it get going) than the breaking strain of your line, and that means you're going to have to let it take line by using the drag on your reel. The alternative to this is back-winding, where you literally wind the reel backward to let the fish take line. I don't recommend this unless you're in real trouble and can't think of anything else, because it surrenders control of the fight to the fish, and anyway, it's such a clumsy technique. If a large fish wants to run and builds up so much power that you can't stop it without breaking the line, then you have to let it run, keeping pressure on it all the time with your rod. Keep the rod high, as this will give you greater overall control and will also allow you to see where the fish is by following the line — useful if it's halfway across the lake!

With extremely large fish, some anglers find that the gentle touch really does work, and that a monster you can't possibly stop with brute force can sometimes be coaxed and cajoled toward the net with light pressure.

LANDING NETS

When it comes to landing a fish, there'll be an anxious moment or two when you have to take your other hand off the rod and reach for the landing net. First, make sure it's within easy reach (and assembled, obviously) and that you've dipped it in the water previously so that the mesh will sink. The important thing is to get the net into the water in front of you and deep enough — you want to draw the fish over the net and then simply lift it so that it cradles the fish. If you have the net too near the surface, the fish will see it and spook. Practice your technique with smaller fish first, or fish with a friend and take turns netting each other's catch. After that, pull the net toward you, grab hold of the frame, and lift the fish out of the water with that, rather than using the handle.

Safely in the net — larger fish may need to be held gently in the water to recover.

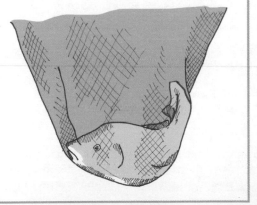

CHEATING

Anglers have long had a bad reputation for exaggerating their piscatorial successes. Indeed, the phrase "the one that got away" has passed into general usage. This is entirely unfair, as I intend to prove below.

As a group, anglers stand before the rest of the sporting world with a genuine sense of grievance. Golfers drop balls from their pockets onto the green when the actual ball lies lost in the trees half a hundred yards away. Boxers take bribes, horses are doped, hockey players try to hit seven bells out of each other with large crooked sticks, gymnasts starve themselves, sprinters take steroids . . . but it's anglers who get the nudge, nudge, wink, wink treatment. We simply don't deserve it.

Yes, I really did catch this cod down at the village pond, and no, I didn't know they came ready battered, either.

"Get that down the fishmongers, did you?" sneer the unbelievers, never mind the fact that not even the most exotic food hall is going to stock bass or pike, since neither are exactly valued for the tastiness of their flesh (think cotton ball and needles). Facts are powerless to stop the innuendos from flying, though. In fact, I'm convinced that the reason so many anglers bring fish home in the first place is to silence their spouses.

Then there's the equally unfounded feeling that anglers exaggerate their successes by increasing the length, girth, and overall numbers of the fish they catch. Seriously, why would anyone want to do this? It's not as if the skill of angling is held in high regard (in the general public's imagination it probably sits in a slot somewhere between shepherd and washroom attendant), and it's not as if being a good angler is going to help you find a partner on a Saturday night (would that it did). An angler has no reason to cheat because he has nothing to gain — certainly not the respect of his fellows, who can spot a phoney a mile off. Fishing may be based on deception, but in my experience those who practice it are generally honest.

There's a lateral-thinking problem that goes like this: A man is crumpled in the bottom of a phone box, dead, the windows on either side of his body smashed, a bloody arm dangling through each one. The receiver swings from side to side and a voice comes out of it: "Hello? Hello?" How did he die?

A: He was an angler, of course, on the phone to a friend and raving about a fish he'd caught. "It was THIS BIG," he said, forgetting where he was and spreading his arms out enthusiastically. They smashed through the windows, which cut his wrists, and he bled to death.

FLOAT·TUBE FISHING

Even if wading gets you close to the fish, it's still got plenty of limitations in places where the surface area is too large or the water itself is too deep. Sure, you could use a boat, but not everyone can afford to buy one or has the means to get it to the water, so wouldn't it be great if there was something in between? There is. Meet the float tube.

The float tube is essentially a souped-up rubber ring. You inflate it, climb in, wade out to the point where you start to float, and then kick off as if you were a kid learning how to swim. Once you're afloat, you'll find you can fish spots that the shore angler can never get near.

Did I say it was like a rubber ring? Well, sort of. There are a number of different designs, from the traditional "belly boats" that look like a tiny kids' inflatable paddling pool with a hole for your legs and blow-up arm- and backrests, to the U- and V-shaped ones which are much more like inflatable armchairs and allow the angler to sit higher in the water. Modern ones use multiple bladders (for safety), have copious storage compartments, fluorescent safety "accents," somewhere to put your coffee cup — the full nine yards.

FLOATING AWAY

You'll need some extras to take advantage of a float tube, notably neoprene waders and fins so you can keep warm and move about easily. Remember that you'll always be moving backward in a float tube, and that, unless you use one of the specialized anchors, you'll always

be drifting around the lake. In fact, since you have to move your legs in order to stay still, you should limit your first few trips to a couple of hours each until you get the hang of it. You should also make sure that key bits of tackle — like your tackle box — float, and that you wear a life-jacket.

By the way, you should probably prepare for this to become an obsession. Float-tube anglers are completely mad for it, and many see it as the single most liberating thing they've ever done in their angling lives (probably because it neatly combines fishing with messing about in little boats). Make sure that you start on a still water before progressing to rivers, and always make sure that float-tubing is allowed. Anglers in warmer climes have an advantage over the rest of us, but with proper clothing, anyone can enjoy float-tube fishing.

The common float-tube angler (Piscator armchairibatus) at rest in his natural habitat — a trout in one hand and the remote in the other!

THE ANGLER'S CAR

Unless you're in the exceptionally fortunate state of being able to afford a separate automobile for your angling trips, there's probably no such thing as the perfect angling car. All you can do, then, is make your ordinary one fit for the purpose.

Most cars are used for many purposes and have to cater for you, your partner, the family (if and when that arrives), as well as accommodating various substandard hobbies that have nothing to do with fishing. You'll probably have to fit some bits of furniture in there at some point as well. Given the Transformer-style qualities that are required of the modern automobile, the best you can hope for is to sneak small corners of the car for yourself in the hope that no one notices.

At the minimum, the car must be big enough to take your fishing rods. If it can't, then it barely has a right to be called a car at all and you should change it immediately. If you're the kind of angler who likes to transport their rods in large bags ready made up, you'll need

a roof rack and plenty of bungee cord. Assuming the car can accommodate the rods in some way, then it'll also have the remaining features you require, and even piddling little hatchbacks can carry enough gear for three anglers and their luggage for a week's vacation.

ORGANIZING

Get one of those strong, plastic "bags for life" from the supermarket to keep your rubber boots in, and stuff a spare pair of thick socks inside the boots. I also keep a pair of thong sandals in the car to change into when I get wet feet — the heater inside the car keeps my toes plenty warm enough. I keep an old waterproof waxed cotton jacket in the trunk, along with a pair of shorts and a T-shirt for emergencies, as well as canned corn and one of canned meat for those days when I forget my bait. If I could afford it, I'd keep an entire travel-rod kit in there just in case. If I used a big fold-away seat, that would stay in the trunk as well, along with a spare flashlight and a bottle of water. If you're the forgetful type or you don't have any decent pockets, you can keep your licence, membership cards, and permits in the glove compartment.

Even an ordinary hatchback car can be pressed into service as an angler's car — though perhaps the occasional application of some air freshener is advisable.

UNHOOKING A FISH

As soon as you have a fish out of the water, either in a landing net, in your hands, or on an unhooking mat, you have a responsibility to remove the hook from that fish as quickly and efficiently as possible.

The first thing you can do to make life easier for you and the fish is to use a barbless hook. Under tension, this holds just as well as a barbed hook, but it comes out with a lot less hassle. Barbed hooks are outmoded and cruel, and, along with live baiting, should be consigned to angling's garbage can.

If your fish is lip-hooked in the rubbery part of the mouth and it's plainly visible, you may be tempted to try to remove it with your fingers. Don't. Even under the best of circumstances you're unlikely to get the leverage required to remove the hook first time — when you add wind, rain, dazzling sunlight, a fish that doesn't understand what you're trying to do, bankside mud, and slippery fingers, you're onto a loser. Instead, use a pair of fishing hemostats. These will allow you to get a good grip on the shank of the hook and ease it out with a smooth curl of your wrist. The long-nosed versions can reach a good way down a fish's throat, too, and are excellent for removing hooks if you can see what you're doing.

USE A DISGORGER

If you can't see what you're doing and need to remove a hook by feel, you'll have to use a disgorger — a slim metal or plastic rod with a slit and a nick at the business end. Slide the line into the slit, wind the disgorger around the line a couple of times and then slide it down the line, into the fish's mouth, until touches the eye of the hook. You'll

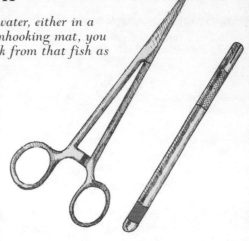

Hemostats and the traditional tube disgorger are both essential tools for anglers who are interested in the welfare of the fish they catch.

then need to roll the disgorger delicately between your fingers until you can push the end over the eye of the hook. Once set, you can push down to remove the hook and carefully pull it out.

Sounds difficult? Don't worry. The beauty of this method is that you can practice it. Tie a hook onto a piece of line, hook the business end into something, and off you go. To make it more realistic, try using a length of see-through plastic tubing such as a drinking straw. To make it easier, try gripping the line about a foot away from the fish's mouth to keep it taut. If you don't have a spare hand, use your lips to hold the line rather than your teeth so that you don't damage the line. Keep practicing as well, because unhooking a fish well is an important skill to learn — just as important as being able to catch it in the first place.

MAKE YOUR OWN BAITS

Sure, you can fish with ready-made baits like bread and worms, or buy specially concocted ones like banana-flavored luncheon meat, but there's nothing quite like the thrill of catching a fish on a bait you prepared lovingly with your own two hands. Here are some simple recipes.

HEMP PASTE

Hemp seed has been known as an excellent bait for years, but not many people make it into a paste so that it's suitable for going after larger fish like carp and catfish. It also has another distinct advantage: eels don't care for it.

+ First prepare your hemp by soaking it in cold water for a day, then boiling it until the seeds split. Drain and then leave to cool.
+ Mash the seeds into a thick paste, then add a bit at a time to about a square foot of rolled-out pastry.
+ Be careful how much you add. If it gets too sloppy it won't stay on the hook.
+ One other thing: the hemp you get from a pet shop may not be as good as the more expensive stuff that tackle shops sell — it doesn't split for some reason — so buy a small amount first to check it out.

CHEESE PASTE

The bait that has it all. You can make it any color you like, give it different consistencies for different conditions, and make it good and smelly.

+ Take some ready-made pastry (about a square foot), grated cheese, cheese flavoring, and blue food coloring (blue is more easily seen by fish at depth than most other colors).
+ Sprinkle the cheese on the sheet of pastry, add a dozen drops of food coloring and the same of cheese flavoring.
+ Fold the corners of the pastry into the middle to make a rough parcel and then knead the lot until all the ingredients are mixed.
+ You can freeze this and use it as you need it.

Cooked hemp seed also makes attractive loose feed

Despite the cannibalistic connotations, most fish love trout pellets

Cubed meat is a classic bait with wide appeal

Cheese paste — the bait that has it all

TROUT PASTE

A deeply unpleasant concoction that stinks of fish. It's a strange old world when the fish like to eat stuff that smells (and probably tastes) of themselves. But like it they do, so here's how to make it.

+ Get a couple of pints of trout pellets and crush them up. There's no easy way to do this unless you buy a cheap food processor. I tried driving over a bagful in my car once, but just got pellets all over the road – and when it rained . . .
+ Next, mix with a couple of raw eggs until it makes a stiff paste.
+ You can also add the oil or juice from tinned oily fish like mackerel or sardines, if you can stand the stench.

CURRIED LUNCHEON MEAT

Here the key is in the cooking process, which not only binds the flavorsome curry powder to the meat but also toughens up the skin so it stays on the hook better and resists the attentions of smaller fish.

+ Cut the meat into cook-sized cubes and then roll them around in a bowl that has two tablespoons of curry powder in the bottom.
+ When the meat is coated, fry it quickly in a little oil until it starts to go brown – this will ensure that the curry flavor binds to the meat.
+ Again, this can be frozen in bags until the night before you go fishing.

BREAD PASTE

An old-fashioned favorite, this regularly accounts for larger fish than more common baits like maggots.

+ Use old bread — a couple of days at least — because it's harder to get the lumps out of fresh. I don't know why. Trim the crusts off and then dampen, but don't soak, the bread.
+ Squeeze out excess water.
+ Wrap the paste in a clean, white cloth and knead away — using a cloth like this stops your greasy hands from discoloring the bait.
+ If you want to pep up your bread paste, add some instant blancmange mix — strawberry or vanilla is good.

MEAT PASTE

Useful when the fish have become suspicious of perfectly formed cubes of meat (another dodge is to tear off chunks of luncheon meat rather than cutting it up with a knife).

+ Get a couple of standard-sized tins of luncheon meat and put them in a food processor (a cheese grater will also do if you need the exercise). Place the resulting mess in a large mixing bowl.
+ Make yourself a hot cup of instant gravy or yeast extract if you prefer, stirring thoroughly to dissolve it in the hot water.
+ Pour this into the bowl with the meat and then add flour to the mixture a little at a time until you achieve the right consistency.

HI-TECH BAITS

There's no end to the baits you can make for yourself at home, and that's without getting into all the modern appetite enhancers, enzymes, minerals, and other goodies that some anglers employ. You can find out more about those on pages 86 and 87.

PERMISSION TO FISH

There are few things more exciting than discovering a piece of water that's not only new to you but also looks as though no one else fishes there. This immediately opens up all sorts of possibilities — more specifically the prospect that the fish will lack the caution of those pursued more regularly.

I've always found the best way to locate new water is to buy a topographical map and study it, or hang around in the bars that anglers frequent. Both methods have their advantages, but although the bar is certainly more fun, fishermen have a tendency to blather and over-elaborate, and anything they say should be taken with a pinch of salt — usually one from a bag of chips.

Locating a new water is only half the battle, however. If it's privately owned, you must persuade the owner to let you fish it. With the right approach and the right conditions, people are just as easy to catch as fish — here are a few tactics I've found to be useful over the years:

+ Ask around the local area first — has anyone ever been allowed to fish there, did the landowner's daughter run off with an angler, and is he handy with a shotgun?

+ When you knock on the door or ring the bell, take two steps back and stand relaxed with your hands at your sides. Smile. You'll look less threatening.
+ Don't turn up on someone's doorstep in full fatigues and carrying all your gear — you'll frighten them off.
+ If they seem uncertain, try to think of something you can do for them in return — small lakes and ponds are often left to run wild and the owner may like the idea of having someone tidy up a bit.
+ Explain that it's only you who is asking to fish and that you're not the vanguard of an angling horde waiting in a bus down the lane.
+ Explain that you'll treat the water and its surroundings with respect and would be happy to limit your visits to a mutually agreeable number each year.
+ Only offer money at the end when all else has failed.
+ Most importantly, remember to ask if there are any fish in the water.

If all goes according to plan, you could end up with your own private lake or stretch of river. If that's the case, it may be worth trying to secure it on a more formal basis by creating a small syndicate to fish and manage the water. This is a genuine revenue earner for the landowner, and therefore very attractive. Above all, be polite and always take no for an answer if it's clear they mean it.

THE MAIL-ORDER FISHING KIT

It's the boy's introduction to fishing, the terrible first rod-and-reel combo that — like a nasty initiation that nobody ever speaks about — lies in wait from the moment you say you want to go fishing and see what all the fuss is about.

The first thing to say about fishing kits is that you probably shouldn't. Your typical telescopic rod with its selection of peculiar and singularly unusable floats, weird spinners that no one else wanted, swivels (but nothing you can attach to them), and hook-to-nylon lengths of indeterminate provenance and reliability provide a poor start compared with what you can get by having a quiet word at your local tackle shop. You may pay slightly more, but it'll be worth it to end up with a setup that you can actually use to do some proper fishing.

There are mail-order companies that offer total fishing kits that include a tent and the whole ball of wax, which is OK if you want to go camping rather than fishing! Shops still selling rod-and-reel combos in long semi-stiff see-through plastic bags sealed by a single snap at one end should be reported immediately. They are going to a very special level of Hell . . .

Despite what the picture implies, it's very unlikely that the owner of one of these would ever give the thumbs-up about fishing. Save yourself some heartache and avoid.

THE FISHING BAG

This is among the most personal of possessions. It must contain everything you need to help you meet every single angling situation in any of the four seasons, as well as carrying all of your sandwiches and a flask. Impossible? Of course. Stupid bags.

I've tried lots of bags. I once bought a backpack/stool that lasted only until I demonstrated it to my wife in the store car park and ended up on my backside, legs waving in the air. That went back. I had a brand new leather bag, which lasted a season and then fell apart in front of my eyes in a single afternoon, leaving me to carry all my gear home wrapped in a jacket. I had an old gas-mask bag, which served for many years and still does for overseas trips. I then bought a wicker creel, which was so expensive that I don't dare change it for anything else, even though I can barely fit anything inside. In desperation I've tried going fishing without a bag at all, but that's just a mess and everything you wear ends up slung so low it looks as though your pockets are full of beer cans.

🐟 TYING A FLY

Never mind a book, you could probably fill an entire bookshop or small library with books on fly tying, and even then, experts would shake their heads gravely at the disappointing and cursory way in which the subject that's so close to their hearts has been dealt with. They're going to love these two pages!

I'm not sure why anyone would want to tie their own flies. I mean, it's not as if there's a shortage of pre-tied flies out there, with desperate anglers queuing round the block — so it must be about something different. I suppose as your skill grows you may feel that you can do a better job than the manufacturers, who are at least as interested in keeping the unit cost down as they are in matching a particular fly, but I suspect the motives are rather different.

Anglers love to fiddle about, adjusting this and that bit of tackle, then adjusting it again relative to another bit, then adding something, taking it away again, before starting all over from scratch.

Fly anglers are even worse because successful fly fishing is about so much more than whether your chosen fly actually resembles the thing it's supposed to be imitating. I've seen enormous trout caught on flies that looked like something you'd pull off the sleeve of an old coat because it was irritating you, or bizarre mutant The-Flies-Have-Eyes things that scared me, let alone the fish.

So I suppose it must be like making your own bait or perhaps your own beer. Better still, your own wine. There's no way you can hope to match a prize-winning Merlot or Shiraz, but if your Old Elderflower can catch while others fail, imagine the satisfaction.

TOOLS OF THE TRADE

If you want to get into fly tying you'll need some specialist gear. You can substitute some of the materials involved, but you need a decent vice to hold the hook in place. This can be screwed onto a bench or table. They key thing to watch out for here is a vice that can grip small as well as larger hooks — cheaper vices don't give such good grip on small hooks.

The main tools of the trade are a couple of pairs of sharp scissors with fine points to get into tight spaces and

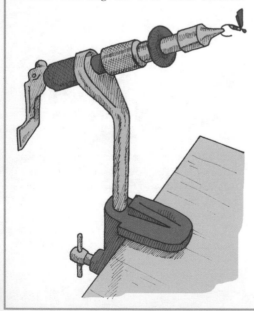

A fly-tying vice is essential. It will grip large and small hooks alike, as well as rotating so that material can be wound around the shank of the hook more easily.

trim off excess material; I'd recommend two because one of them should be used exclusively for tougher material like tinsel, and these babies need to stay sharp. You may also find it useful if the tougher one has a serrated blade. The other main tools you'll require are hackle pliers for gripping and winding, a bobbin holder for applying thread, a whip finish tool for completing the fly, and a dubbing needle for picking out dubbing or applying varnish. This being fly tying, there are literally dozens of other tools I've missed out, but these are the essentials.

Although the materials listed here are widely used for fly tying, there's really no limit to the strange things that can be used to make a fly. In fact, if it has substance, you can probably use it.

FLY MATERIAL

When it comes to fly-tying materials, you can be as experimental as you like, but there is a wide range of threads, furs, and fibers that are recognized all over the world as being up to the job:

+ Tying thread — usually nylon and in any color you like, though brown, olive, and black are the most common.
+ Wool — which is good for putting some bulk on your fly. Chenille, that weird caterpillar-like (hence the name) wool, works well.
+ Tinsel — this is now plastic-based, so it doesn't tarnish and adds a tempting luster to your fly.
+ Dubbing — once made from fur (rabbit and seal are good), this is now just as likely to be polypropylene or some other man-made fiber.
+ Dubbing wax — makes the thread tacky so that you can apply the dubbing more easily.

+ Cock hackles — plucked from the necks of chickens to provide the hackles for all kinds of flies.
+ Feathers — all kinds can be used to create bodies (and sometimes wings) of various nymph and dry-fly patterns.
+ Floss — one made from rayon is very good for creating a body that tapers.
+ Head cement — for sealing the head of the fly and stopping the threads from unwrapping. Also provides a glossy surface for painting.

METHOD

There's no correct way to tie a fly (there probably is, actually) but there are plenty of places where beginners can get help. Your local library may have books on the subject with step-by-step guides, or you can buy interactive tutorials that run on a computer, or an instructional video. You may also find classes in your area where you can learn with others. This is undoubtedly the best option since it will also introduce you to those who share your curious obsession!

Finally, unless you have exceptional eyesight, you'll need good glasses or some kind of magnifying glass and a decent dose of direct light. Much of the work of a fly tyer is very fine, and it's easy to strain your eyes.

GHOSTS

It's inevitable that when you spend so much time in lonely places at the end of the day or through the long hours of the night (or what J.R.R. Tolkien called 'the cold hour before dawn'), strange things happen. In a way, it would be even stranger if they didn't.

Water seems to attract ghost stories almost as much as it attracts anglers. There's the spooky estate lake, of course, nestling in the woods, candle-light flickering in the windows of the gatekeeper's lodge far away, the sound of a woman weeping by the boat house, distant laughter away among the trees, and foxfire there at your elbow. But it's the same on the towpath beside a city canal, where tall shapes loom in the fog and a sudden cold spot takes your breath away as you walk through it. Or on the banks of the village pond where a dog lost years ago still howls for its master.

BUMP IN THE NIGHT

There's always stuff going on where water and land bump up against each other — two elements sharing a similar space, trying to accommodate the anglers who move between them. If you've fished alone through a night, you'll know what I mean. There's always a moment when the world turns and everything around you adjusts itself ever so slightly and becomes unfamiliar and a little unsettling. I'm sure that's why some anglers make so much noise at night — whistling past the graveyard and all that.

Some ghosts are explained away more easily than others. The rustling in the woods is usually an inquisitive rat; the heavy footfall along the bank is your companion coming to scrounge some bait; the sudden chill is what happens when the sun goes down. Others are harder to deal with — a vixen crying in the dead of night is an astonishing sound, like nothing else on this earth.

Is your favorite lake haunted? I can think of worse places to hang around after I'm gone, if I'm given the chance. It might be entertaining to check out a few old friends, wander off into the middle of the lake to have a look at the snag where I lost a 20-pounder in '04, poke around a bit, maybe set a few bite alarms off or fire up an outboard motor . . . you know, just for fun. Anyway, I always fancied myself as a bit of an angling legend.

A haunted lake, the dead of night, a solitary angler — what could possibly go wrong?

PHOTOGRAPHY

All anglers like to look back and reminisce about the fish they've caught but, while in the past it wasn't uncommon for a large fish to find itself stuffed and mounted in a glass case, these days the angler's commemorative weapon of choice is the camera.

I have neither the will nor the skill to turn you into a crack photographer, so I'm not going to bother. I will say this, though: unless you're a complete computerphobe, get a digital camera. Anything above two megapixels is fine for the kind of snapshots most anglers want, and they're pretty much bombproof when to comes to taking decent photos.

If you're fishing with a friend, then photography is pretty easy. Making sure that your hands are wet so as not to damage the mucous membrane that helps prevent infection, you should cradle the fish just under its head with one hand and at the end of its back near the anal fin with the other.

Some anglers hold their fish up by the gills with the mouth facing the sky. Don't do this. Make sure you hold the fish low and over the unhooking mat or a patch of soft grass so that if it does wriggle free it won't have far to fall. Hold it away from your body as well, so it doesn't get damaged by any sharp bits and pieces that may be attached to your clothes. This also has the beneficial by-product of making the fish appear bigger.

SOLO PHOTOGRAPHY

When taking a picture on your own, I'm not a big fan of timer photographs, unless you've got a proper tripod. Setting the camera up on a tree stump never works for me, and there's a danger you'll end up wasting too much time trying to get the picture right while the fish is gasping

A nicely composed photograph of a prized fish. Handled with care, this is the best way to remember the occasion.

in the net. Instead, gently pull the fish's head and tail out from the folds of the net so it's lying on top. Position the rod and reel above the fish (and maybe add a float or something else small). This frames the fish and also gives the viewer a sense of scale.

As you stand over the fish to photograph it, lean over more than you think you should and you'll actually get a better flat-on photograph. Return the fish to the water as quickly as you can take the picture, and if things aren't going well photo-wise, skip it and get the fish back anyway.

THE FISHING TRIP

It's a time-honored ritual where anglers can bond together away from the pressures of work and the responsibilities of the family and relate to each other on a primal level — how many fish can they catch, and who's going to catch the biggest?

I'm going to talk about men going fishing together, because that's what I know about — a women-only fishing trip is likely to be an entirely different kind of beast, probably far more stressful and certainly twice as competitive.

First, let's define what constitutes a trip in the first place. It has to involve traveling to a new place and staying away from home, and should take place over a weekend at least, preferably longer. You need to stay somewhere — a tent, camper, trailer, hotel — and have some opportunity to socialize away from the water. Otherwise it's just a long fishing session. Remember: even a fishing trip shouldn't involve too much fishing, so build in breaks, outings, and so on, and try to engineer at least one occasion when some of your party return late to their lodgings the worse for drink and without their keys — it's expected.

Finally, it really isn't advisable to go on a proper fishing trip with people you've never met before (the exception is an exotic expedition abroad, where you get what you're given). Everyone should know at least one other member of the group — it'll help the group dynamics.

MIX AND MATCH

There's no "right" number for a trip. I know some anglers who swear by even numbers, arguing that people instinctively pair up and this stops anyone feeling left out (it also helps with hotel bills if you can share a room, more of which

The group of anglers preparing to begin their annual fishing trip all had the same unspoken question: Who invited Father Christmas?

below), but I've never seen any particular advantage. Anyway, it's the composition of the group that counts rather than the precise number of people.

Most of the group should be generally easy-going, but it never hurts to have someone with a bit more get-up-and-go who can winkle people out of bed the morning after a heavy night and support the ongoing fishing efforts with local bait suppliers, maps, permits, and so on. People to avoid include feuding brothers, newly-weds, and anyone who's just given up smoking.

If you're traveling by plane, give your luggage the once-over. Chances are you'll have to buy some rod tubes, and since these are rarely over six feet (1.8 m.) long, there may not be room for a favorite two-piece 14-footer. Trying to take a fishing bag on as hand luggage is going to delay you, your party, and everyone else on the plane while airline staff try to sort out what all those weird gadgets are for. Instead, put your fishing bags in with the main luggage. Bed-chairs and other large items should be bungee-corded together and wrapped in thick plastic bags.

SLEEP TIGHT

An interesting dilemma is always posed by accommodation, mainly because the most cost-effective way to run a trip is to have people sharing rooms. This is a very peculiar notion for grown men to come to terms with (think about it — the only men who regularly room together are either servicemen or sportsmen), and no matter how well you think you know someone, their bed-time routine and general nocturnal habits are likely to raise a few eyebrows. The quirks may be surprising but harmless – not being able to go to sleep without the radio on, always leaving the window open, keeping the TV on standby because they like the way the little red light winks at them. Others may be worse. Most hotels don't allow smoking in rooms, but after dark there's usually the odd enterprising angler leaning out the window for a crafty puff. If you've got a snorer, try to keep them off the booze and stagger the times you go to bed. Take your sleeping arrangements seriously — for a sport that requires you to stay still for so long, angling's a tiring business.

(It's not all bad, by the way. I once roomed with an angler who made up a bedtime story for his daughter every night of the trip and recited it to her over the phone. Best week's sleep I ever had.)

EACH TO HIS OWN

If you're driving to various locations, have designated drivers and rotate them so everyone gets a chance to snooze in the back. Remember to purchase the appropriate level of insurance. Don't leave any good stuff in the car, either, because organized thieves have been known to target anglers and are partial to tackle, iPods, expensive fishing jackets, and, of course, the car itself.

Vary the fishing to suit the different members of the group, and don't force anyone to do something they're not comfortable with or equipped for. Fly-fisherman don't often enjoy ground-baiting for catfish by hurling buckets of blood and offal into the water, because it stains their Gore-Tex. By the same token, don't stereotype anyone in the group — encourage people to branch out.

Finally, on your return, get someone to open an account on a free Internet photo-sharing service like Flickr (www.flickr.com) so people can post their pictures for everyone in the group to see. This saves you all making photo CDs and posting them to everyone.

A good rod tube is essential for the traveling angler, to ensure that you don't set off with a two-piece rod and arrive at the water with a five-piece.

FISHING MYTHS

All sports construct their own mythology, but the stories surrounding fishing are rich and varied, universal, yet absolutely personal. And like the best mythology, it's alive today and waiting for you to make your contribution.

First, there's always the myth of the monster fish, which I've dealt with in more detail on page 38. However, there's one special subset worth mentioning here, because all the fish listed before are desirable creatures — fish that you'd actually go out of your way to catch. There's one fish, however, that ticks all of the other boxes and deserves its place in the pantheon of fishing myths: the killer fish.

Every big lake has one of these: a mutant predator of such proportions that it can gobble down a passing labrador. "Oh, and by the way, did you hear about that poor kid? He went out beyond the ropes and disappeared. All they found was the remains of his inflatable ring washed up in the bay over on the far side. Covered in teeth-marks it was." This kind of story is useful when you need to deter packs of small boys who are determined to swim where you are fishing.

WATCH OUT . . .

Another good one is the bottomless hole, somewhere in the lake. It's often part-covered by an ancient rotted mattress, which only makes things worse since you won't be able to feel the hole beneath your boots until it's too late. Our local one had such a pit, and the story was told of the cow that wandered across the pond in one of the hottest months of the year, only to slip and drown. When the water level rose again, the bottomless pit remained, but now with an extra helping of cow.

Taking time out from the daily grind of fetch-the-stick to get a drink, Spot is unaware that he's being followed.

Most lakes have hidden quicksand somewhere around their margins, impossible to detect and — funnily enough — often where the best fishing is also found. Kids, it's always best to listen to an adult in these situations.

Have a go at creating your own myths — after all, that's how the cycle perpetuates itself — and don't be concerned about making them too outlandish. Anglers are generous (all right, gullible) souls and will usually give the teller of the tale the benefit of the doubt. Which reminds me, I must phone the club secretary and get him to close the main lake. I'm sure I saw a dark shape in the woods there last night as I was packing up. Probably one of those giant cats. Or a bear. Better safe than sorry.

EVERYONE ELSE

Unless you're fortunate enough to have a private water all to yourself, it's likely that you'll have to share your peace and quiet with others, who may not be as interested in silence as you are. Most water users can rub along together pretty well, but inevitably there are going to be moments of tension. Here's what — and who — to watch out for.

The single thing that works against an angler the most is stillness. If you're good at staying still (I had a mink emerge from the water and run over my foot once), many other water users won't see you until they're on top of you. In the past I've been run over by an off-road cyclist, got tangled up with a huge guy in a canoe (he was as quiet as me — a deadly combination), had sticks thrown into my swim for dogs to chase, been woken from a daze by four kids dive-bombing into the water in front of me from the opposite bank, and got bumped in the back by a sleepy cow coming down to the water for a drink. (To be honest, I'm usually so pleased at being hard to spot that I don't mind the ensuing abuse.)

EXCUSE ME . . .

Thus, it's usually up to stealthy anglers to take steps to warn other water users that we're about. Anyone on foot can be warned off by a casual cough. I've got quite good at this over the years, and can usually measure the volume so that it's loud enough to warn the intended target, without disturbing the overall quiet of the day. This also gives dog walkers a chance to get the beast under control before it makes off with your bait, sandwiches, wallet . . .

I've been on the wrong end of boaters more times than I care to recall, and have come to the conclusion that there's only one way to treat them, and that's to behave as if you're on a bicycle and they're in an SUV. You can engage in a debate (i.e. hurling insults across the water at each other) about how everyone's got a right to use the water and how they should consider the needs of others, but in the end you're going to need to reel in unless you want to lose 50 yards of line and all that expensive end tackle. You can always catch up with them later and drop a few worms into their fresh-water tank. No, I didn't say that.

Divers haven't proved much of a problem to me thus far, but then I usually fish small rivers that are shallow.

Boats are more difficult to manoeuvre than you might think. Make sure you reel in before there's a chance of tangling with one.

MAKE A MINNOW TRAP

Given that I'm against live baiting, some readers may wonder at the purpose behind making a minnow trap. Well, it's fun, it's something to do with the kids, and there's an undeniable pleasure in looking at these beautiful little fish. It'll take you back, too.

Slide the smaller bottle into the larger one

Make sure that the tops are facing in the same direction

There are lots of different ways to make a minnow trap — you can even pay good money for one, and I don't mean the fancy antique ones — but this is one of the simplest and most effective. All you need is two large plastic bottles (two-liter ones will be fine), a pair of sharp scissors, a stapler, a large nail, and something to hold it over the heat with. Oh, and some string or fishing line.

Start by cutting the bottom third off the first bottle with the scissors. Next, cut the top third off the second bottle. What you should have ended up with is two-thirds of an original bottle with the top intact (we'll call this bottle 1) and one-third of the second bottle, also with the top intact (bottle 2). If you haven't, buy four more liters of soda, drink them, and start again.

Unscrew the top of bottle 2 and place it inside bottle 1 so that their necks are pointing in the same direction. This gives you an entrance (bottle 2) that is very easy for the minnows to swim into, but very hard for them to find their way out of. Secure the two bottles together with staples all the way around the edge.

Hold the nail over a gas flame with a pair of tongs or something else that's safe to use. Wear an oven glove if you want to, and if you're a kid, have an adult around to blame if it goes wrong (I mean, to supervise). When it gets hot, use it to poke 10 holes all round the outside of the trap, so that it'll sink. Tie the string or

Keep an eye on your minnow trap. Small fish swimming around in a confined space will inevitably attract larger fish, and a pike is perfectly capable of biting through bottle plastic to get at the good stuff inside.

fishing line around the top and then pop a few bits of bread inside. Sink the bottle in a likely spot and leave it for a couple of hours. Retrieve the bottle, unscrew the top and you should be able to pour your catch carefully into a jar.

You can't keep them for too long because they need running water, but they're great to show to kids and are fascinating to watch for an hour as they dart about. And with the record minnow currently standing at only 24 grams, there's always a chance you could . . . you know . . .

THE FOUR SEASONS

"There's no such thing as bad weather," goes the old adage, "only bad clothes." I feel the same way about fishing, and you'll find me on the banks when the banks aren't banks any more because they're underwater, or when they've pulled back from the river during a drought, standing high and dry like teeth in receding gums. Each season has its own pleasures, and I love them all.

I don't understand people who won't go fishing when the weather's foul or the conditions are awful. They're missing some of the best bits. The tiny panfish you catch quiver tipping when you can't feel the nose on your face, let alone the tug on the line, is far more satisfying than the stupefied carp that made you put your can down on a lazy summer's evening because it cruised by your floating dog biscuit and couldn't be bothered to close its mouth. A love of adversity is part of what makes us anglers.

I remember going to a favorite river in the January floods in search of chub and discovering that the water-to-land ratio had altered rather drastically since my last visit. I still caught one, and better than that I caught it at the spot where I normally retire to have a crafty pee when water levels are more manageable. Priceless. He was a lovely chub, too, and full of fight.

Ray and I have fished with ice on the rings of our rods — knocking them against the bank every so often to get rid of the frost and make sure the line can run freely — and we've still caught a fish or two. Not so many, maybe, but there have been hours of great companionship in knowing that we tried, and, shuffling back to the car like two old frozen scarecrows (one wearing brightly colored snow boots), we've known the simple joy of feet being slowly warmed by a spluttering car heater.

I don't really have a favorite season. The fall, maybe, because that's when the river is at her best, but I also love June and the way the summer and its long evenings seem to stretch out interminably ahead, so full of promise. I keep meaning to fish on Christmas morning, but I don't quite know how to swing it with the sheriff (my wife). Unless it was more of a symbolic thing for an hour — a few casts at a favorite corner (I know just the one), with perhaps the kettle for company. I might not even take any bait.

The Fifth Season

I save this description for those odd days that are completely out of character with the ones that precede and follow them — a freezing summer night, for example, or shirt sleeves on New Year's Day.

PROVISIONS

Man can indeed live by bread alone, but usually prefers the odd piece of cake, bag of chips, chocolate, or packet soup in order to keep going. Particularly important during an all-night session, provisions can make the difference between a successful trip and one that ends, you know, the other way . . .

Like most things to do with fishing, it starts when you're a kid, just as it did in the playground or cafeteria when you sat with your friends and gingerly opened your lunchbox to see what lay inside. What followed was sometimes disappointment, sometimes outright joy (especially on your birthday), and more usually the start of a swift bartering session with your schoolfriends. On the riverbank there's rarely the luxury of swapping with anything other than the fish — and personally I'm convinced that fish have developed their love of luncheon meat from thousands of unwanted sandwiches lobbed into rivers and lakes over the years.

WHAT'S IN YOUR LUNCHBOX?

Whatever your home situation, there's inevitably a point in your life when you start making your own lunch and discover that eating hunched on the bank isn't quite the same as eating anywhere else. For example, you need to think about how you're going to hold your food with those maggoty hands (pasties have that pastry ridge for a reason, you know — that's where tin miners used to hold them while they scoffed the rest). Unless you're centered enough to reel in and take a proper break, you need to have something you can get rid of quickly in the event of a bite. Food left on or near the ground has the ability to galvanize slugs into mega-mollusc levels of speed, and the thought of chomping into a ham sandwich that has an unseen guest attached doesn't bear thinking about.

Elsewhere, there are other special circumstances to consider. I've had my dinner snaffled by a passing dog, and frozen anglers begging hot drinks until the Thermos was empty. Consider, also, that if you eat everything in your bag by 10:00 A.M., you usually can't replenish your supplies. The worst of all, however, is the moment when you open your bag, find that there's nothing there, and after a second you can see — clear as day, in

A typical angler's lunchbox (actual lunch, bought from gas station on way to waterside, not pictured).

your mind's eye — the little plastic box of goodies sitting on the kitchen counter, exactly where you left it.

FANCY A DRINK?

If you're staying for any length of time, you'll also need something to drink. Keep it simple: water in the summer and a hot drink in the winter. Limit yourself to no more than the odd beer, no matter how tempting it is. There will usually be a point sometime during a trip when you need all your wits about you — and anyway, you'll usually have to drive home in the end. Drinking and fishing make poor companions — if you want to spend some time outdoors having a drink, go to a music festival instead.

A Thermos is fine for a quick raid, but there's nothing quite like a fresh hot drink, so think about a little camping stove or a Kelly Kettle (see page 26). This is also good for boiling water to rehydrate those dinner-in-a-bag meals favored by hikers, and despite the fact that they look like astronaut food (i.e. the same coming out as going in), they're tasty, portable, and easy to prepare.

A final thought: Anglers have a bad enough reputation without adding to it by leaving the remains of your dinner behind. Throw it in for the fish and the waterfowl by all means, but if you want to leave it for the bankside critters, drop it deep into a bush out of sight. Passers-by won't see it, but the animals will find it soon enough. Remember that they don't like aluminum foil, packaging, or plastic film any more than you do.

Patience

If I had a penny for every time someone said to me "Fishing? Nah, haven't got the patience," I'd have enough to buy a new fly rod by now. If only they knew the truth . . .

From the outside looking in, angling can seem like the epitome of the contemplative person's pursuit. All that sitting around apparently doing nothing must, onlookers assume, result in a blissful, good-for-the-soul, Zen-like calm. In fact, as all anglers know, nothing could be further from the truth. Beneath that apparently calm exterior, a typical angler's mind is a-buzz with a million and one things to do with fishing and — believe it or not — everything else in their lives. Thus:

Am I using the right bait? Should I fish the slack rather than the edge of the current? Should I have started earlier? Can I manage an hour after dark? Is the hook completely hidden? Is it too soon for a cup of coffee? What's that noise? Did I check the end of the line for abrasions? Was that a fish breaking the surface there? Where's my wallet? Ooh look, a deer. Did I lock the car? My fingers smell, don't they. Was that a bite? I did cancel that 10.00 A.M. meeting, didn't I?

And people don't understand it when we come home exhausted.

WHAT'S IT LIKE BEING A FISH?

Do you remember in The Sword and the Stone, *when Merlin changes the infant King Arthur into a fish and he's chased round the castle moat by the giant pike? Ever wondered what it would be like to go to bed one night and wake up the next morning as your favorite fish? Wonder no more.*

Waking up is one of the most efficient things you do all day — you don't even have to open your eyes because you don't have any eyelids. Instead, you kind of drift back into focus, or maybe it's more like when a daydream stops. If you've dropped down into the mud or wedged yourself against a tree root, you shake free and start the day.

The first thing you notice is how noisy it is. Since you don't have any obvious ears (and are not a Walt Disney fish), this is a bit of a puzzler. The explanation involves a tiny bit of science. Sounds are essentially vibrations, so you're actually feeling the sounds around you courtesy of a pair of fluid-filled sacs with fine hair-like feelers that send messages to your brain. But that's not all. You've also got a built-in amplifier called a lateral line, which runs down the side of your body and boosts the vibrations. Add the fact that water transmits sound beautifully in the first place, and that's why it's so noisy.

WHAT'S THAT?

Looking around, you realize you can't see very far. This is partly because the water is cloudy, partly because you're fairly deep, and partly because you're short-sighted. Your lateral line starts ringing as something hits the surface above and you instinctively rise to investigate it. There's something there, but it's not until you're higher in the water that you can make out that it's red (this is because colors behave differently in water and red is the first one to 'disappear', while blue and violet remain visible at much greater depths). But there's also all sorts of other weirdness going on, because, like most fish, you can see the ultraviolet part of the spectrum as well.

And what's that smell? Yes, despite not being able to breathe through them, your nostrils — or nares — are incredibly sensitive. As you suck water in, your olfactory bits sift through the various chemical signals and then send the results to the part of your brain that determines what they are.

But enough of all this, here come your friends, so fall in line, don't bunch up at the front, don't lose your place, and make like you all look like one big fish so nobody gets eaten. At least not today.

You don't look like you have the slightest clue what's going on, but in actual fact you're a finely tuned, highly sensitive creature who can hear an angler getting his gear out of the car half a mile away.

SNAGGED

In the early days, when all you catch are tiddlers, there's very little danger of getting snagged up — unless, like me, you're preternaturally clumsy, or specifically target those species who live in the root systems of old willow trees. But when you hook a big one ... that's a different matter.

The best advice for those anglers who fish in waters that have snags is simple: keep the fish away from them. Alternatively, don't fish there in the first place. Unfortunately, most anglers know that fish have a sense about these things (they learn it at snag school) and invariably choose to lay up in spots that offer speedy access to sunken trees, old bedsteads, and dumped, rusting shopping carts.

Set your reel drag so that it gives line grudgingly — if the drag is too loose, you won't have any control over a decent-sized fish. And when you first strike, give it some stick, let the fish know straight away that it's in for a fight and that you're not taking any nonsense. Keep up the tension — especially if you're using barbless hooks — and all will be well.

Of course it won't. You did all the right things and the fish still managed to wriggle its way into the snag on the opposite bank. So what can you do? You've no doubt heard of the total business solution? Well, I'm a big fan of the three-stage total snag solution.

Stage one is where you try to pull the fish out. Don't literally pull it, but pull until you figure you're about 20 per cent away from snapping the line. If that doesn't work, reduce the tension by about another 30 or 40 per cent so you've got a bend in the rod, but there's still some leeway for the fish to pull it over. Then wait. This is the worst bit, but it really does work. Give it as much time

Fish can find snags in an instant, and getting them out requires patience and luck ... but remember that it can be done.

as you can stand — I've waited as long as 20 minutes — and with any luck, the fish will extricate itself from the snag and carry on the fight in clear water. If there's no movement at all, move on to stage three — let the line go completely slack so the fish feels no pressure at all. Wait. You'll be surprised at how often this will encourage a big fish to free itself from a snag. Then, with an evil grin, you can tighten up and start all over again.

PASSING IT ON

Nobody taught me how to fish, and that was fine. I learned in my own way, made my own mistakes, and, by watching those around me and absorbing what I could, slowly became the angler that I am today — flawed, patient, slapdash, inconsistent, utterly focused, superstitious. Frankly, it's a wonder I catch anything at all.

The truth is, if angling has a future — and there are those who say it does not — it's down to today's anglers to make sure that there are enough kids taking it up to keep the sport going. That means every angler has a duty to pass it on, either as an individual, as part of a fishing club, or via various schemes run by agencies such as the U.S. Fish & Wildlife Service (www.fws.gov).

If you plan to teach kids how to fish, then get them off to a good start by providing decent tackle — just because you had to start with a broom handle and a piece of string doesn't mean they do as well. There's something to be said for making do with older, hand-me-down gear once they've got the bug, but to begin with, having a good rod and a reel to match will make your pupil feel good about fishing and help them to persevere when they're not catching anything. Remember, you're competing with an Xbox 360, not a set of dominoes.

ENCOURAGEMENT

By the same token, you need to take them somewhere that's got a good head of fish so that they're going to get bites. They don't have to land anything big to begin with — even the smallest fish will encourage a youngster to keep casting — but it's important that they always feel they're in with a chance.

You'll have to decide whether or not to fish yourself. I've tried it both ways with varying degrees of success, but overall I favor leaving my tackle at home. Having someone who needs help in baiting up, casting, reeling in and playing a fish is a full-time job and I don't want anything to distract me. I find it helps to sit near your pupil and talk to them, especially when there's nothing obvious happening. Kids can be remarkably patient if they think there's a chance of a fish, and the more you give them the benefit of your behind-the-scenes knowledge of what's going on under the water, the longer they're going to stay interested.

Tell them about the fish you've caught, and when they need a break, take them round to other anglers so they can watch what they're doing. Encourage them to ask questions. If you don't know the answer, tell them you'll find out. Teaching someone to fish can be a learning experience for everyone, including the teacher. So pass it on.

THE PRIEST

Although many anglers return the fish they catch unharmed to the water, we're sometimes fortunate enough to catch something that will make a good meal for family or friends. So, if it's a matter of putting dinner on the table, it's important to understand how to kill the fish quickly and humanely.

I have a problem with some of my sea-angling friends who are perfectly decent chaps but are also happy to leave a fish they catch flapping around in the bottom of a boat, gasping for oxygen until it suffocates. It's not right. I know it seems as though the sea — and thus the stocks of fish therein — are limitless, but that's a misconception that encourages anglers to treat fish carelessly. I think it's perfectly acceptable to kill a fish and then take it home to eat — but what's the best way?

WHAM, BAM, THANK YOU, MA'AM

Of all the methods I've come across, by far the most reliable and practical is the "priest" or "fish bat" — a short, heavy club that you use to whack the fish smartly on the head, just behind the eyes. It's important to deliver the blow with some force, or the fish will merely be stunned, which is no good for fish or angler when it comes round a few minutes later and starts slapping

A simple, heavily weighted club made of wood or metal, a fish bat is the most humane way of killing a fish if you intend to take it home for your dinner table.

round the bank. Hold the fish firmly in a cloth and smack it smartly on the top of the head just behind the eyes; if you're uncertain, do it twice to make sure.

Various other methods have been suggested to me down the years, but I've found them either too unreliable, too complicated, or too bloodthirsty to include here.

You can buy clubs (also called saps, coshes, billies, and so on — so many names for something that despatches death) from most shops that sell fly-fishing gear. Simple ones with aluminum bodies and stainless steel heads are inexpensive, but you can expect to pay more for the fancy jobs with wooden handles and heavy brass at the business end. Alternatively, you can use something long and heavy from home. Some trout-anglers' priests double as marrow spoons for investigating the fish's diet — more of which on page 100.

There are various theories as to why it's called a priest. The most convincing is the obvious one: it's used to administer the last rites to a fish and send it toward your table efficiently and with dignity. If you always remember that, you'll be able to fish and take home your catch with a clear conscience — and enjoy it in the same way.

ONE FOR THE POT

Once upon a time, fish was hailed as the healthy alternative to meat. It was richer in essential fatty acids, vitamins, and minerals. It was a lot less cholesterol-inducing than many kinds of meat. It was generally seen as an all-around good thing. Recently, however, some have argued that both sea and freshwater fish absorb too many pollutants to be good for anyone, and should be avoided. Confused? Wait until you add angling to the equation.

It didn't register at the time, but on a recent rereading of Bernard Venables's classic English cartoon book *Fishing with Mr. Crabtree in All Waters*, I discovered it contained at least one observation that set the alarm bells ringing. At the end of another routinely successful fishing trip — how do those line-drawings do it? — Crabtree and Peter have ended up with a handsome perch, whereupon the master says: "There. Isn't he lovely? About a pound. And what a delicious meal he'll make. There's scarcely a fish to beat him for flavor in sea or fresh water. Split open and grilled, he's good, or he can be roasted." Hang on a minute: eat a PERCH?

Of course. That's what English people did in the 1960s, when they knew nothing about fresh swordfish or langoustine, and long before anyone over here had been fooled by the idea of sushi. In those earthier times we were quite happy to take the occasional fish for the pot. And when trout or salmon were hard to come by, there were always pike or Mr. Crabtree's delectable perch.

FAST FISH

Naturally, the practice of eating freshwater fish that aren't salmon or trout has its roots in religion. Originally from Asia, carp were first brought to England via mainland Europe by monks in the thirteenth century. Sequestered from the world they may have been, but the good friars knew a thing or two about scaring up good food for fast days and Lent. Carp being carp, they thrived. They grew fat in their stew ponds on the scraps from the monks' kitchens, came when they were called, and were easy to net.

The notion of eating during a fast is a peculiarly religious one and comes down to their loose definition of fasting.

There are many tasty recipes for cooking freshwater fish, and almost none of them involve putting it on to boil with the head and tail still on.

Rather than abstaining from all food, the monks looked on it as observing a disciplined diet that excluded meat (still seen all over Europe as a rich person's food, because you had to buy it or have enough land to raise cattle of your own) but included vegetables and that other easily obtainable source of protein, fish. Fast days were originally Wednesdays, when Judas betrayed Jesus, and Fridays, when Jesus was crucified. The other big fast was during Lent.

END OF AN ERA

Why did eating freshwater fish become less popular in Britain? Mainly for the usual reasons: high price and poor availability. Add to that the strong, fishy flavor, the fact that most people can't tell a tasty fish from an inedible one, and the desire of people from the 1970s onwards to separate themselves from the sources of their food and eat tinned, packaged, and frozen foods, and it's no wonder the attraction waned.

What's more, even anglers — who are a notoriously slow bunch — could work out that if you ate a fish it would not be there for you to catch the following week, so they put it back. As angling became more popular and the pressure on waters increased, so catch-and-release became the norm.

As far as I can find out, however, it's not against the law to take a fish home and eat it. Individual fishery owners and riparians may threaten those who practice catch-and-consume, but I believe the most they can do is either ban the offender or possibly try to have them arrested for theft.

Now until recently, none of this has been much of a problem, but with the opening up of the European Union

Fishing for Starters

As a boy, I was aware of a time when groups of ladies who would normally be seen taking tea together or attending the opera were said to have held gudgeon-fishing parties on the river Thames at Windsor — with a view to eating their catch. The scene can scarcely be imagined, and it always struck me as a rather exciting development. It's odd the things that tickle the imagination of a young boy as he sits on the riverbank.

come workers from countries where it's acceptable — even traditional — to eat freshwater fish like carp, pike, and tench. Indeed, in Germany, Poland, and the Czech and Slovak Republics, carp is the centerpiece of the traditional Christmas Eve feast, so it's no wonder that they've got their eye on the local monster. The problem can't be solved with a few signs either, since many of the newcomers have only imperfect English. Add to that the fact that anglers have a blind spot for signs anyway, and it's possible there'll be a few spots of low-level bother. The angling — and even the national — press has been trying to whip this up into a big story, quoting unnamed anglers threatening violence to any Klaus, Ziggy, Laszlo, or Janko that they find wandering away from the bank with a shopping bag full of carp. It's mostly inflammatory nonsense, of course.

Mind you, imagine how frustrating it'd be to pursue a large and famous fish for years, only to meet it for the first time in between two slices of bread.

BAD LUCK

We've spoken elsewhere of the beneficial power of good luck, and how sensible anglers work to cultivate it whenever they can. However, every angler knows that the real key to successful fishing is in avoiding bad luck. So what should you be looking out for?

As I get older there are certain things I avoid, such as fatty foods, bad whiskey, and keep nets. I don't take a keep-net fishing any more, because the last three times I did, I didn't get a bite. Then, the first time I forgot it, I caught my biggest ever fish, so the next time, anticipating another monster, I took the keep net again. Nothing. This continued until even my addled brain could work out the pattern and I sold the net (by then it was bad luck just to have it in house).

BANANA BOATS

Similar uncertainty surrounded the affair of the landing net. I knew it wasn't a question of leaving it behind with the keep net, but should I put it up before I cast or was that being too presumptuous? Like an idiot I tried it both ways, and was only convinced when, having fended off bad luck long enough to hook a good-sized rainbow trout, I realized that it would be impossible to land without the net. Aaargh, bad luck had disguised itself as good luck and then ambushed me. It would take years of spitting on my bait before the first cast, never changing rods while fishing, never telling anyone how many I'd caught, leaving my wallet at home (an easy one, that), and never saying 'banana' on a boat before I'd paid enough penance and was allowed to set up my landing net as soon as I reached the water.

Other rotten talismans? A new camera always brings bad luck, as do new gumboots; a clean shirt is at the very least a bad omen, and the last time I went fishing on Friday the 13th no less than three people round the lake fell in, all at different times and different spots.

Finally, although it doesn't really come under the category of luck — good or bad — it fits with the generally superstitious nature of this page. Fish can sense when you're rolling a cigarette or tamping a pipe, they can hear the sound of a Thermos top being unscrewed at a thousand yards, and decades of evolution have taught them to wait just long enough for the thirsty angler to begin pouring before they take the bait. And if you think that's just bad luck, well more fool you...

Despite having a generally confusing role in the making of good and bad luck, if a black cat turns its back on you . . .

YOUR FIRST ROD

Your first rod is like your first kiss. It's the benchmark by which all subsequent rods (and kisses) will be judged. It sets you off on a path through your angling life and exerts a subtle influence on the techniques you use and even the species you prefer. And if you're like me, you'll probably have several "first" rods.

My first first rod was made for me by my dad. I say "made," but all he really did was liberate a length of bamboo cane from the garden and screw in half a dozen curtain rings, and that was that. We added the cheapest of centerpin reels made from Bakelite (that space-age material from the 1960s), some 6 lb. breaking-strain line and a few floats, weights, and hooks, and I was off. Of course the rod didn't bend at all and the reel barely revolved, so I could swing the end tackle out into the water in front of me, but not much else.

TRYING AGAIN

My second first rod was the result of ignorance and an unscrupulous shop assistant. We were on vacation and my one-piece bamboo rod wouldn't fit in the car, so we went to a local tackle shop and came away with a suitable beginner's setup — for sea fishing! I lived 200 miles from the sea. It was a 6-foot (1.8-m) boat rod with a wooden handle, more suitable for landing sharks than the small fish that lived in my local pond.

It came with that miracle of engineering, an open-face spinning reel, but foolishly I believed that the better angler you were, the heavier your line needed to be, so mine was packed with 14-lb breaking-strain line. It was almost impossible to fish with. The line tumbled off the spool in uncontrollable loops as if the reel was possessed, and tying on a size 16 hook was real camel-through-the-eye-

Remember what they say about fishing tackle: its first job is to catch anglers, not fish. You have been warned.

of-a-needle stuff, but since neither I nor my friends knew any better, I persevered for over a year.

The third first rod was a 10 foot 6 inch (3.2 m) fiberglass two-piece "general-purpose" rod, light enough to do a bit of float fishing, but with enough poke for some ledgering. It was on this that I fluked my first carp, it was my first real fishing rod; and partnered with a Mitchell 324 open-face reel it became the rod of choice of my angling life.

Until my fourth first rod came along, that is . . .

THE ANGLER'S ATTIRE

Although some will argue against it, there's a strong school of thought that believes anglers are the only group of sportsmen and women who have worse dress sense than golfers. I mean, have you see what this year's angler is wearing?

By and large, anglers are unconcerned about their appearance — though, as we'll see a bit later on, there are exceptions to this. If it were possible to teleport to and from the lake or river and then home again, this would be less of a problem because there would be no one to see us but our own kind. However, because the typical angler must travel from their closet to the car (usually via the kitchen) or take (God forbid) public transport, the opportunities for some What-Not-to-Wear-style catastrophes are usually all too obvious.

What the general public (and family members) fail to understand is that of all the lovers of sport, the angler is the one least interested in fashion and most interested in keeping warm and dry. This is the nature of the beast. Very few pastimes require one to go and sit outside in the same place all day, sometimes barely moving for hours at a time — and you'd better believe we want to be comfortable.

WHO'S WHO

This opens the doors to all manner of mix-and-match sartorial experiments, and results in our lakes and rivers being populated by people who look like well-behaved vagrants. The fact that anglers are drawn from all parts of the social spectrum — and that the universally

What the well-dressed angler is wearing this year — except anglers rarely are well dressed. Whatever your style, opt for layers to keep warm.

awful clothes mean you can't tell the bank clerk from the busboy — only adds to the fun. I well remember meeting a man on an obscure branch of an exclusive stretch of trout stream who looked like he'd spent the afternoon asleep in a bush. We fell into the most interesting conversation about fly tying, and as we reached the last gate I offered him a lift. He replied that he was fine, thank you very much, and disappeared round a large stand of trees. I shook my head sadly and assumed he was bedding down for the night, got into my car and drove off. Moments later he overtook me, driving what appeared to be a Rolls-Royce Silver Spur III Armored Touring Limousine. One of only 91 ever made, if memory serves.

As for practical advice, angling is like camping in that the secret to staying comfortable is to use layers of clothing in order to trap the heat, topped off with a light, waterproof — and breathable — outer layer, or shell, to keep the rain off. Gear from an ordinary outdoor shop will fare as well as specialist angling or sporting clothing, and costs a lot less. And the beauty is that it doesn't matter what you look like. In fact, the more outlandish the better.

SOLDIER ANGLERS

Now to the exceptions. When it comes to clothes, sports anglers are actually golfers who arrived late, joined the wrong line, and signed up by mistake. They enjoy brightly colored clothes (even when it's clear that the fish do not) and are in love with technology. For clubs and golf carts, just substitute fish finders and motor boats. Soldier anglers, on the other hand, would like to be hunters but don't have the opportunity — or the nerve — and so compensate by dressing up as bushes and trees and crawling along the banks, even when it isn't necessary. Most of the time I can't look at them — all that camouflage just makes my head spin. Give them their due, though — they are hard to spot. In fact, I'm almost certain that I sat on one once, had a few casts, caught a rainbow trout, and then moved on. The man never moved an inch.

Although there may be some advantages to army-style camouflage clothing, I've yet to be convinced it's superior to wearing muted colors.

Disgusting Baits

When it comes to real filth and gore, freshwater anglers simply don't compete with their sea-loving counterparts. That doesn't mean to say they don't try, though . . .

Clearly, the larvae of flies and other insects are pretty unpleasant, as are worms of various descriptions, but really these are standard fare that shouldn't deter even the occasional angler. Slugs are a different matter, thanks to the industrial-strength slime that won't come off your fingers or clothes or anything else it touches (it's surely the stuff that Spiderman squirts out of his wrists), and all sensible anglers cultivate a technique whereby they can hook the slug without actually touching it.

When it comes to baits to make your eyes water, however, you have to defer to the catfish angler. Raw hamburger mixed with Shredded Wheat and garlic powder, anyone? Hotdog marinated over a hot summer's night in a large glass of cola? Chicken hearts mixed with gizzards, with some juice from oily canned fish? Offal stewed in pig's blood and then mashed with bran to make slimy balls? Given their diet, it's no wonder that catfish look like that.

🐟 FISHING FROM A BOAT

For many people, the idea of combining angling with messing about in a boat is pretty much pleasure personified. You get the excitement and tantalizing anticipation of angling, with the more straightforward fun of getting into a boat and playing around.

Of course, the most important thing about fishing from a boat is to be safe. That means you need to be able to swim, you need a life-jacket of some description for everyone in the boat, you need more than one person who can make the boat work, and you shouldn't go out in a boat on your own. Oh, and you should tell someone when you're going out in a boat and arrange to call them when you get back. That way, if you don't they can then raise the alarm and come and save your sorry backside.

Keep clutter to a minimum in the boat. Share essentials like a landing net with your companion, have a central store of bait, ground bait, and so on. If you've never been on a boat before, have a little practice in the shallows. In particular, rehearse standing up to pee over the side, as this is a skill you will certainly need to acquire.

Although boat fishing is traditionally seen as a way to cover large areas of water by trolling, spinning, or fly fishing, it's also fantastic for reaching those little tucked-away spots that no one ever visits. You should thus resist the temptation to make your way immediately to the middle of the lake, and instead look closer to home for your sport. Fish love to patrol the margins, and also the shelf around the edges of a lake where the bottom drops off into deeper water. Plumbing the depths will help you find out where this most productive spot is to be found, so you can set your tackle accordingly. You'll be surprised at how many fish you can catch from a boat close in.

Keep the noise and moving around to a minimum and you'll find that this allows you to fish surprisingly close to the boat without spooking them. This makes boat fishing great for beginners who aren't yet able to cast very far. Finally, remember the old saying that "it's always an overcoat colder" in a boat than it is on shore, and dress accordingly. Layers are best because you can remove them, but the top one should always be lightweight, breathable, and waterproof. Only take an umbrella in a boat if you don't mind losing it over the side.

Fishing from a boat allows you to get at places that shore-bound anglers can never reach, and then fish them in comfort. Make sure you take proper safety precautions.

CLEANING A TROUT

Part of catching and eating your own food is preparing it properly. If you've never gutted and cleaned a fish before, you may be anticipating a bony mess. This isn't necessarily the case, but you should probably conduct your early cleaning sessions in the yard, just to be safe.

For this you'll need a trout (of the correct size, according to whatever the regulations say you're allowed to take home) and a sharp knife. Some chefs recommend a short bladed knife, but in my experience it doesn't make a lot of difference. A little spoon is useful, too.

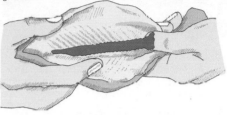

You can remove the blood or kidney line with your finger or thumb by running it along the inside of the opening.

Off we go. Wash your hands. Place the trout on its side on a chopping board with the head pointing away from the hand you favor (i.e. if you're right-handed, then the trout's head should be pointing to your left). Take the knife and pop the skin at the anus with the point. Be very careful not to push the knife inside beyond the tip, or you'll tear the sac inside and this may taint the flesh of the fish. Continue cutting until you reach the throat. Scoop out the guts with your fingers (or with the spoon if you're feeling sensitive) and discard them. Inside the cavity you'll see a thin red line running the entire length — this is the blood or kidney line and it needs to come out as well. Use the spoon to remove this, and throw it away.

Saw off the head just behind the gills and chop off the tail where it joins the body. Then, instead of washing it clean with water, wipe it down thoroughly inside and out with a damp cloth. This will help to preserve the flavor.

You can cook the trout like this on a barbecue or put it in foil and bake it in an oven. Alternatively, you can have a go at filleting it. This is hard to describe, and you're probably going to mess it up the first few times — I know I did. Have

a look at what's left of the fish, lying on its side. What you want to do is slip the knife between the ribs and the outer flesh, getting as close to the ribs as you can. There are various techniques that recommend you to start at one end, or at the top, or to go round clockwise or whatever. I start at the head, and kind of "rock" the knife along the rib cage until I reach the tail end. It works fairly well most of the time.

Good Eating

The best fish to eat are undoubtedly trout and salmon, and I don't eat any other kind of freshwater fish. I have a peculiar relationship with so-called game fish, and don't mind eating them in the slightest. When it comes to bass, pike, and carp, however, I can't bear the thought.

READING THE WATER

One of the wonderful things about fishing is that it's a mystery, a never-ending puzzle that requires a dedicated and perceptive angler to solve it. And one of the biggest mysteries of all is discovering what lies beneath the surface of the water itself. So where do you start?

You begin to read water by accident. By chance you come across a spot and start fishing there because it's attractive or because it reminds you of a photograph (perhaps one that also had someone in the foreground holding a large fish) or because it's close to the parking lot, or has some other practical appeal. So you set up, start fishing, and you have a good day. The next time you visit that water you go to the same place because you figure that what worked once may well work again — and damn me if it doesn't. That's when you start looking more carefully at the water in front of you, and that's when — like one of those stereogram pictures that appear at first to be just a swirl of colorful dots — everything suddenly becomes clear.

RUNNING WATER

Fish are predictable. Unless they have a specific reason for doing otherwise, they will always face upstream. They may relocate from time to time for a better view or some other fishy reason we don't understand, but they'll always return to that upstream position. That's because the food comes from that direction. Anything washed down the river, or rolling along the riverbed, comes toward the fish that are facing upstream, and therefore they can see it coming sooner and more clearly. How does this help the angler? Well, sitting there in the current takes a lot of energy, so fish will sidle to one side and sit in slack water slightly out of the current so that the food either comes close to them or they can drift out into the main current, grab something, and then drift back into the slacker water again. You can see where faster and slower waters meet because there'll be a "crease" in the water. This is nearly always a good spot to try.

Look for obstructions: fallen trees, accumulated autumnal rubbish that's hooked onto low-hanging branches to form a canopy, long, flowing ranunculus weeds, large rocks, that kind of thing. Fish will lie up behind these — they do interesting things to the current, often slowing food down and swirling it round so it's easier to grab. Even if you can't actually see anything, the condition of the water will give the game away. Look for unexplained bulges and pockets in the surface of the river.

If the surface of the river in front of you is smooth and flows more evenly than the water above or below it, you could be looking at a nice hole in the riverbed. Plumb the depth of the entire stretch and then fish either at the top or bottom end of the hole. Fish love these spots because they can rest up away from the main current, yet still receive a steady supply of food.

Similarly, look for eddies — where the water actually flows against the main current direction, usually because of an undercut bank — and bends in the river where fish will lie up in the deeper water out of the main current, waiting for food.

Finally, dam pools are fantastic spots for holding fish — the main pool itself, the slack, deeper water further downstream, and then the shallows below that. Dams stir up the bottom of the river and swirl lots of interesting particles about, which provide a steady supply of food and encourage fish to start feeding.

STILL WATER

Lakes and ponds can be trickier to read than running water because there's no obvious current bringing food to the fish (unless it's a stream-fed lake, in which case you'll often get good fishing around the spot where the running water comes into the still water). However, on larger lakes watch which way the wind is blowing, as the fish will follow it to the downwind edge and feed off the food that's been blown over there.

In lakes you need to find features like gullies, inlets, and bars, all of which will attract fish. Lilies and reed beds in the margins are also great holding spots because of the insects that live there. Such spots will also bring in predators who feed off the smaller fish. Mapping the bottom of the lake is difficult without a boat, but there

Left: Fish love reed beds because they provide both cover and a supply of food. Fish as close as you dare.

Below left: Obstructions in the river provide natural breaks in the current, and fish will often lie up behind them, picking up bits of food.

are specialist bobbers that can help, and you can also do it yourself. Tie a weight onto the end of your line, cast out and, as the weight hits the water, trap the line with your finger. Then release it again, counting out one-Mississippi, two-Mississippi and so on, allowing ten feet (3 m.) for every second. If this is too time-consuming, try to get to the water when the level is low — some of the features normally under water may be revealed.

The other foolproof way to start reading the water is to watch other anglers. If they're catching lots of fish, watch what they're doing and where they cast, and go and talk to them about it. We're a friendly bunch on the whole, and often happy to share a tip or two.

Above: Lily pads are good spots to find fish and usually indicate shallower water — watch out for their tough roots, though.

THE EMPTY NET

In England it's called "blanking." It's a strange expression, as if it's only the presence of a fish that gives a trip any definition, and that when you don't catch anything, the event itself is empty — as if nothing had happened at all.

Becoming an angler is all about living with failure, so it's a good idea to get used to it. Someone once said that in angling, unlike other sports, your opponent is essentially nature itself — unpredictable, ever changing, and infinitely patient.

It's infuriating. You can go to a water one week, fish a lure on the surface and get arm-ache from reeling the fish in. Go back the next week with the same conditions, at the same time of day, with the same chop on the water and the same lure, and you'll get nothing — not so much as a sniff.

Because we serve such a capricious mistress, it's important to get a few things straight. First, you can have all the angling knowledge in the world, the finest tackle, the juiciest baits that science can enhance, and the most perfect conditions imaginable, and still the fish won't bite. Sometimes you can fix it — a bait switch, a change of rig, altering the depth or the rate at which the bait falls in the water. And sometimes you have to accept that you're doing everything right and the fish are just being ornery.

ACCEPT YOUR FATE

On occasions like that, you have to understand that this is just part of the you-versus-nature game and get on with it. Move somewhere else, try something else (just promise you won't take up golf), switch things around. Be resourceful. When none of that works, come to terms with the fact that there's more to going fishing than catching fish.

If you concentrate on fishing well, even if your net is empty you'll have the satisfaction of a job well done. At the same time, if you're doing everything right, you stand a better chance of catching a fish, even if it's by accident. Once you accept that, you'll also understand why one person can go fishing, catch nothing, and still come home happy, while the person next to them looks ready to beat seven bells out of someone — anyone — because they've had such a crap day. Don't fall into that trap. Fish well, and then you can get skunked with dignity.

To some anglers, a dry, empty landing net is the saddest sight in fishing — except, perhaps, the sight of their own reflection in the mirror on returning home at the end of another long, fishless day.

CARING FOR YOUR REELS

A reel, even a modern spinning reel, is a thing of beauty, a marvel of engineering, and should be treated with respect, even if it only cost you the price of dinner for two at your local steak house. Sshh . . . they can hear, you know.

I treat my reels abysmally and they've never let me down. That's the beauty of modern mass-produced technology — once the manufacturers get it right, then, boy, do they get it right. None of my reels cost more than dinner for four at the aforementioned steakhouse (with wine), and as I say, none of them has been singled out for any special treatment. I keep each in a soft little bag, sluice them off with a spray of water, followed by a wipe with a soft cloth when they've been borrowed by more brutish friends to go fishing off the pier, and that's about it.

Some manufacturers recommend that a reel be taken apart once a year, oiled and greased, and then reassembled. Since this is something I wouldn't want to do (I've seen the exploded diagrams of a reel, thanks very much), I've never done it in 35 years of fishing — and I've never been tempted to pay someone else to do it either. Unless you are punishing your reels in some way by using them in extreme conditions for very large fish, I wouldn't bother.

Were I to care more deeply about my reels, I'd give them an annual once-over, spraying them with WD-40 (or another silicone spray), adding a few drops of light machine oil to the bits I can see that should be moving, and smearing on the odd glob of reel grease/lube on anything else. (However, before I did that, I'd read the manufacturer's instructions to make sure I hadn't bought one of the new breed of modern reels that have a drag

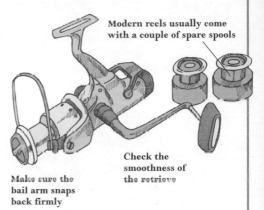

Modern reels usually come with a couple of spare spools

Make sure the bail arm snaps back firmly

Check the smoothness of the retrieve

system that can actually be damaged by being lubricated.) Then I'd wipe the lot with a dry cloth. At the same time, I'd change the line for fresh, ensuring that I didn't overfill the spool but kept it about an eighth of an inch away from the lip.

One thing I always do is give the reel handle a few turns after I pack up, in case some grit or small stones have snuck in between the spool and the housing. You should catch this kind of thing quickly before it can do any damage. Treated with only marginal respect, even a cheap reel will give years of service.

Center-pin reels, by the way, are an entirely different kettle of fish and need proper maintenance according to the manufacturer's instructions. You can usually gauge the relative health of a center-pin by giving it a good spin with your hands and seeing how long it takes to stop; it'll be longer than you think.

HI·TECH FISHING

In their never-ending quest to land bigger fish, anglers are availing themselves of a new and secret — so far as the fish are concerned, anyway — weapon. Technology has arrived in the tackle box, and it's changing the way we fish.

Reading this book so far probably leads you to peg me as a technophobe. Nothing could be further from the truth. This book was written on a notebook PC, transferred to a big Dell desktop via USB stick for editing, and then e-mailed to the publisher; proofs were checked on screen as PDFs before being signed off. When I'm not doing this, I write articles for computer magazines, and in an unexpected synchronization of technology and fishing, you'll find my angling blog regularly updated at www.adurman.blogspot.com. I've got technology credentials coming out of my ears.

TECHNOLOGY TOO FAR

And yet I remain unconvinced about technology's place in angling, and I wonder how far things have to go before other people agree with me. Let's look at a few examples where the anglers' craft is being made redundant by hi-tech gadgetry.

+ Finding fish. On pages 82–3 we talked about reading the water, or 'watercraft' as it's sometimes called. But why bother when for a few hundred dollars you can buy a fish finder to do all the hard work for you? These devices work from a boat or on the bank, and allow you to dispense with such old-fashioned, low-tech tools as your eyes, or even worse, your experience, and just find the damn fish straight away. Smaller ones fit on the wrist, have backlights so they can be used in the dark, and can find fish to depths of 1,000 feet (300 m.). Why would anyone want anything else?

+ Preparing your bait. For a while now you've been able to buy baits and additives that will make fish feed even when they're not actually hungry, courtesy of ingredients called appetite enhancers. In the same way that kids will eat sweets and chips (and burgers and pizza) until they're ready to burst — and certainly long after they've stopped being hungry — so the fish hoover up these things even when they don't want to. No wonder so many of the bass you see are short, squat, and enormously fat. Now it's gone a stage further and you can buy bait that uses these bite-inducing additives and tops them off with a sex pheromone

In the early days, electronic fish finders were garbage. Now, they work very well. But they're still garbage.

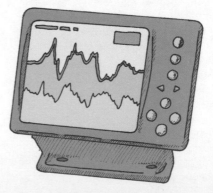

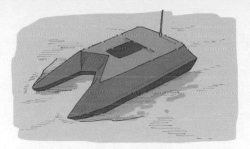

that is apparently so irresistible it's been suggested frenzied fish will eat anything they find in the area that's been baited up — including stones. Just imagine those shoals of fat, horny catfish all homing in on your bait, unable to resist its chemical charms. . .

+ Getting the bait to the fish. Can't cast to that tricky spot on the other side of the lake under the trees? Lost too many weights by casting into the snags either side rather than in the channel between them? Don't bother improving your casting, because you don't have to. Buy a bait boat instead. These ingenious battery-operated, radio-controlled devices allow you to ferry hook, bait, and loose offerings out to the most can't-get-near-it spot and then at the flick of a switch open the bay doors and drop their contents almost silently into the water. Accurate and easy to use (though expensive), these allow anglers access to previously unfishable spots.

+ Attracting the fish. You can now avail yourself of lures that use various technologies to make themselves more attractive to fish. There's nanotechnology, which is being used to coat lures so that they remain highly visible at all angles. You can buy battery-powered lures that flash on contact with water, ones that buzz or vibrate, and others that emit fish-dazzling sonics. Most extraordinary of all are the fish "activators," which reproduce the sounds and vibration of small fish in extreme distress, thus attracting predators. You attach one to your boat, drop the speaker over the side and start it with a foot switch. That's right, you don't even have to get up.

I could go on, but you get the idea. Now it seems to me that gadgetry is fine in its place, but when it takes the unpredictability out of something, when it removes the need for guile and craft, then fishing becomes a bit like getting money out of a cash machine — you just turn up, punch in a few numbers, and out come the fish.

I've heard anglers claiming that a fish finder is the only thing that gives them a sporting chance when they're off for a weekend's adventure fishing in unknown waters. No it isn't. Ask the locals, find a farmer, go to the bar. The answers you get will be at least as reliable, and finding them will be ten times more fun, I can guarantee it. Technology, schmechnology.

THEM INDOORS

The Irish playwright George Bernard Shaw is supposed to have said that "Behind every successful man, there is a woman." Fair enough, but what most people don't know is that the quote continues: "And behind every unsuccessful man, there are two." All I know is that there's a family supporting every lifelong angler — whether they like it or not. And fair play to them.

When you're obsessed, you need help, and not the kind of help that "cures" you of your obsession, either. No, you need to feed the beast, and it's usually up to family, friends, and roommates to help with the ingredients. At the start, it may seem that a drink, a sandwich, and enough money for a bag of chips is all the help you'll ever need, but pretty soon you want more. You need space for an extra rod or two, somewhere to store your wet net and rubber boots ("I can't store them in the shed, they'll get damp," you argue with an addict's addled logic). Then it's a lift to your buddy's house, or to the train station, or to the lake — at 5.30 in the morning. And even that's just building up to the big one: storing your bait in the fridge. "You won't even know they're there . . . "

BAIT BATTLES

I've known partners fall out over this one, especially when the bait in question is alive and the bait box has a loose lid, resulting in what's known in angling circles as "an unrequested larvae–refrigerator interface event." Mine got out on the train once, which was quite spectacular, though I felt unable to hang around for the main event as I assumed that, due to my attire and fishing tackle, suspicion would fall unfairly on me.

Unless they fish themselves (Fish Family Robinson?), it's hard for family members to get it, especially if you don't bring back what you catch for the table. Any support in the face of this impossible-to-square circle is above and beyond the call and should never be taken for granted. So when you come in, keep the stories to a minimum, wash your hands straight away, deposit fishy clothes in the washing machine, keep baits and wet nets outside, shower and change, and rejoin whoever it is that you live with. Give them chocolates or wine or whatever you give them when you want to show your appreciation. They've done their part by letting you go fishing, now it's time for you to do yours.

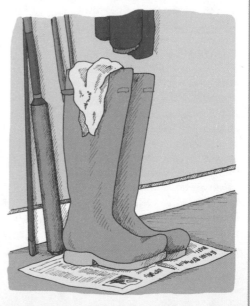

KEEP NETS

As a youngster, one of the high points of any fishing trip was the moment when the keep net was removed from the water and its contents displayed on the bank. It was the totting up of the head count, the final ritual that made packing up almost bearable. And it's not something I remember with pride.

I blame the media. They made it fashionable to measure your success in terms of a netful, and we used to keep fish all day even when we didn't own a camera. Back then, keep nets didn't use modern micromesh either, and fish — especially the small fish we used to catch — would routinely get caught in the holes as they tried to swim to freedom. Clumsy, uncaring boys' hands could usually free them eventually, but by then the damage had been done and it was commonplace to see half a dozen small fish out of a net of 20 or 30 floating away upside down on the surface after the net had been emptied. Our keep nets would be attacked by pike, too, from time to time, but we thought that was a good laugh in our shallow, bloodthirsty way — like watching a shark attack, close-up.

Cramming fish together in a net does them no good. There's no reason to keep any fish longer than the time it takes for a photo and to let it recover before release.

No Thanks

I stopped using a keep net 10 years ago now, though not, I'm ashamed to say, because of some sudden piscatorial epiphany. Instead, it was because I became convinced that taking a particular one fishing was bringing me bad luck. Impressive, eh? Still, unless you're fishing in a competition, I recommend you do the same. Were they able to, I'm certain the fish would thank you for it. It's traumatic enough to be removed briefly from the water, without being held with lots of other fish of various sizes (big ones invariably damage smaller ones), before being tipped onto the bank for photographs, after which the angler scuttles round the bank trying to scoop all the fish back into the water.

If you must use a keep net, separate out small and larger fish (or just return the small ones straight away), and if you catch a lot of fish, consider putting out a second keep net to spread the load. Don't put single large fish in a keep net at all. Use a special sack instead — it's more fish-friendly. But really, think about whether you need to keep the fish at all. I don't miss my keep net. It's less to carry, and I get more pleasure from knowing the fish have been returned speedily to the water.

THE MARGINS

When you first arrive at a new water, whether it's a river, a small stream, a secluded pond, or the largest of lakes, your challenge is always the same: where in all that expanse of water are the fish, and how are you going to catch them? The answer may be closer than you think.

By being stealthy and fishing close in, it's often possible to surprise very large fish and catch them right under your rod tip — and when it comes off, it's exciting stuff, too.

As a boy, I was always impressed by extremes — who could hold their breath the longest, run the fastest, pee the highest, belch the loudest (steady, girls, I'm already spoken for), so when it came to fishing, I naturally wanted to cast the furthest. It's the sort of chest-beating fishing that young, impressionable boys do when they're starting out.

Boy, was I ever wrong. To this day I can't remember when or why I first tried fishing in the margins — the two or three feet (60–90 cm.) closest to the bank — but as soon as I did, I realized I'd struck angling gold. Fish love to patrol the margins, grubbing about for bits of food that have been washed up against the bankside or crumbled from the bank itself. On hard-fished commercial fisheries, where a lot of bait gets thrown into the water during and after a session, there's plenty of food to be had. On rivers, too, you'll catch fish amazingly close to the bank, where they feed on worms, slugs, and insects that have been washed into the water.

SSSHHHH

There's also an interesting by-product of fishing so close to the shore. You learn how to be quiet, how to move as little as possible, how to have a conversation at the level of a whisper, and as you fade into the background, so the fish become bolder and more confident. I caught my biggest carp on floating crust at my feet. I'd been fishing the deep water by the island — like all the other anglers — but as the wind dropped and evening set in I noticed an awful lot of knocking going on in the reeds to my right and left. I threw in a few bits of bread right at the edge of the reeds and waited. Sure enough, after a few minutes I saw a couple of carp working their way down the reed bed. I baited up with a large piece of crust, and dunked it once into the water at my feet to give it a bit of weight for the underarm cast, and as I let it soak, a large mouth appeared from nowhere — right at my feet — and snaffled it.

THE NEIGHBORS

So fixedly do we concentrate on what we imagine is going on under the water that we occasionally forget the many creatures that live on or beside it. They know all about us, though.

Of course, anglers are predisposed to think highly of all nature's creatures, but there's necessarily a hierarchy (eagles and deer near the top, rats propping up the bottom) and many bankside dwellers don't sit terribly high up it. That doesn't mean they're not good value, however. Take a first-timer night fishing, for example, and wait for the yelp as they lean down to grab a new piece of bait only to find themselves engaged an unexpected tug-of-war with a ferocious and highly territorial rat.

I remember a trip to a small pond in early spring. It backed onto a deep wood and wasn't much fished. We crept to the water's edge, tackled up, and fished into darkness. When the torches came out, they revealed that we each had two bats hanging upside down on the ends of our rods, claws locked around the carbon fiber. We lay there, chilly under inadequate blankets, wondering what to do. By the time we'd figured it out, we were, like the bats, fast asleep.

Hi, I'm Rattus norvegicus and I'll be your vermin tonight. For starters and main course, I'll be stealing your bait, and for dessert I'll leave droppings all over your sandwiches.

Where it All Began

All anglers recognize the resonance of particular places, but nothing rings our bell quite so loudly as the place where it all began. That's why it's important to return at least once to that sacred spot, if you can.

Latchmoor pond is virtually dried up now, and I can walk on solid ground where I used to wade up to my thighs and catch tiddlers using a matchstick for a float and bread for bait. Round the back there's no sign of the enormous floating log we used to sit on, having clambered along the treacherous fencing that hung out over the water, all the while waiting for the shouts of "Clear off!" from the yards behind, or the barking of a dog. I caught a huge (for a boy) fish here, and over there a pike . . . 35 years ago now.

We used to hide in the trees when it rained, or when we wanted to share a smoke away from interfering adults. We had keener eyes in those days and could sit hunched on the ground watching our floats, the rain dripping off our noses, then dash across the gravel path when they were pulled under.

Twenty-five years later, on my dad's birthday, I stood on the banks of that pond and proposed to my wife. Now that's what I call a catch.

RAY'S BITE ALARM

Someone once said to me that the electronic bite alarm was like the death penalty — you were either for it or against it. Proponents claim it's the only thing that makes a very long session or an overnight stay possible, and that without one, you'd nod off. Opponents think it's just anglers being lazy.

The "lazy-angler" camp views bite alarms as part of a style of fishing where you arrive with rods already tackled up, and then set up camp, cast out, set the alarms (which detect moving line as a fish pulls it off the reel), and go to bed.

Noticeably, both the for and against views end up with the angler falling asleep. To me, this attitude seems peculiar — like setting an alarm before love-making so that it wakes you up when things start to get interesting.

Fishing should engage you, even when there's nothing happening. Not only that, but being dragged out of sleep by the sound of expensive electronics is no way to catch a fish. Instead, fish shorter sessions. Arrive a couple of hours before dark, fish into the night, and then reel in and go to sleep properly for a few hours. Alternatively, go with a friend and you can keep each other awake.

MAKE YOUR OWN

If you must use a bite alarm, make one of Ray's. It uses a tinkling bell instead of an electronic buzzer, and it doesn't need any batteries. It works in the dark as well, and best of all, anyone can afford one. (Ray claims he didn't actually invent it, by the way, but I don't know of any better, and it's certainly the only one of its kind that I've ever seen.)

All you need is a metal tent stake, a short stretch of very strong line, a small bell on a spring (the kind that birds in cages like to play with), and a hair grip. Put it together as shown below, stick the peg in the ground, then cast in, pull some line out between the reel and the first ring, and pop the hairgrip over it. When a fish bites, it pulls the line and rings the bell. When you strike, the line pulls out of the hair grip and you can then play the fish. If you're using it at night and would like a visual indicator as well, attach a little glowing beta light to the line nearest the bell.

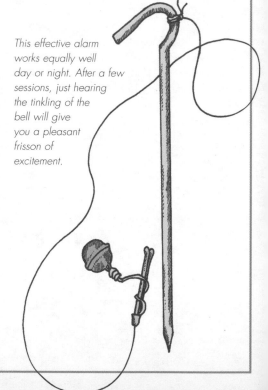

This effective alarm works equally well day or night. After a few sessions, just hearing the tinkling of the bell will give you a pleasant frisson of excitement.

IN DEFENSE OF ANGLING

Although it hasn't been subject to the kind of scrutiny that's faced by other forms of hunting, there's no doubt that angling is on the radar of the animal rights movement. So do we have a leg to stand on?

I was going to research and then talk through some of the scientific arguments about the key issue — whether or not fish feel pain, and whether angling is therefore cruel — but I've tried and I can't do it. The evidence is hard to understand in any meaningful way and I have no way of knowing whether one piece of research is any more or less valid than any other — and unless they're a scientist, neither has anyone else. This means that, for me, the argument is reduced to a level of debate that's barely more sophisticated than "Yes they do" and "No they don't." Anyway, this isn't abstract. This is about me putting a hook into a fish and then pulling it to the bank and then letting it go again; it's personal and deserves a personal response.

Here's what I know. If fish feel pain in the same way that you and I feel pain, then I'm afraid we don't have a leg to stand on. Fishing is cruel, and no matter how we try and justify it, our arguments are merely self-serving garbage.

Here's what I know. I caught an 8 lb. (3.6 kg.) barbel one evening from a stretch of fast water in the south of England and got so excited I went back the next day, whereupon I caught the same fish again — same spot, same

Until such time that it can be proven definitively that fish — like humans — feel pain, we should continue to angle with a clear conscience.

bait, same distinctive markings on its flank. I don't understand why a traumatized fish would feed again so soon and so freely (it wasn't exactly a hard-to-miss bite).

Here's what I know. A famous angler once said to me that were he to become convinced that fish felt pain, he would try to adapt his tackle so that he could continue to fish without actually using a hook. He reckoned he could come up with a way of attaching a bait so that when the fish took it, he could strike, feel the weight of the fish for a moment or two as the fight began and then nothing as the fish made off freely with the bait. For him, that first moment of contact was the touchstone of his angling life, and if he could continue to fish only in that way, then he would.

Here's what I know. Angling runs like a bright thread through the center of my life, and until such time as I am convinced that it is cruel I shall continue to fish as if my life and my freedom depended upon it. In a strange way, I sometimes think that they do.

🐟 BAITING UP

Anyone can throw in a few bits of bait in the vague hope that it will attract fish to the spot and then get them feeding, but proper chumming is an art in itself, and one that's worth spending a little time getting to grips with. By mixing it properly and adding bits of whatever it is you're planning to use as bait, you can introduce the fish to the idea that their dinner is on the table.

Although we'll go on to look at the finer nuances of chumming, or groundbaiting, in a minute, the central purpose of baiting up a spot remains the same, no matter what you're fishing for and regardless of what kind of groundbait you use. You want to attract fish — preferably the right fish — into an area of water that you can cast to, and then keep them there, without overfeeding them so they become uninterested in your hook bait. You may also come across something called pre-baiting, which involves laying down chum in an area before you fish there — sometimes the night before, but also often days ahead — in order to get the fish used to feeding freely in that particular area. Pre-baiting is also good for introducing a new bait to a water and getting the fish used to feeding on it. The big drawback of pre-baiting is that you can spend a week carefully preparing a spot for the big day, only to turn up and find another angler there. Ah well. Wish them luck and move on.

TOOLS OF THE TRADE

✦ Although you may think you can do without one, you really do need a mixing bowl to make proper chum. Get a collapsible one that doesn't take up much space but still has a large, flat bottom — this is the key to a good groundbait bowl, because it makes it easier to remove lumps and get a good mixture that crumbles the way you want it to. It also needs to be round so that clumps of whatever you're using don't get stuck in the corners, because there aren't any.

✦ The chum itself can be simple breadcrumbs, shop-bought crumb that's been enhanced with extra flavors, powdered cereals, mixed particles, additives like bloodmeal and hemp, and combinations thereof.

By using a round bowl with a flat bottom for making groundbait, you'll find it easier to make a crumbly mixture with no lumps — though it may take a bit of practice.

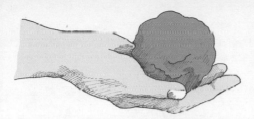

A ball of chum needs to hold together enough so you can throw it, then crumble on contact with the water or when it hits the bottom.

+ Start by mixing the ingredients dry, and then slowly dribble water into the bowl, mixing as you go. Keep working the mixture until you have something that's the consistency of damp breadcrumbs.
+ Leave the mix for about 10 minutes, work it into a ball (adding a little water if necessary), and then either throw or catapult it into the water.

CHOOSING A CONSISTENCY

What consistency should you be aiming for exactly? Imagine a chum scale that runs from sloppy through stiff to powdery. Broadly speaking, groundbait at the powdery end will break up as soon as it hits the water, introducing a slow-sinking misty cloud that will attract fish into the area. Then, because there's very little obvious there to eat, the theory goes that the fish will investigate more thoroughly, until they come across your bait. The disadvantage of chum like this is that you can't throw it very far without it falling apart and scattering over too wide an area.

Stiffen the mixture up and you'll be able to lob it further, but it may not completely break up until the groundbait hits the bottom, where it will crumble to form a little hotspot that fish find irresistible. A slightly sloppier version is good for fishing fast rivers, as the groundbait will hold together until it

hits the river bed. After that, the current will pull bits off so they roll temptingly downstream (obviously, you need to feed the balls of chum upstream of where you're going to fish).

Bait manufacturers have introduced some interesting variations on standard ingredients to produce mixes that "fizz" on contact with water. These mixes hold together well so they can be thrown greater distances, but when they come in contact with water a chemical reaction occurs and they hiss and bubble, releasing gases and stirring things up.

Adding some of your hook bait to the groundbait mix is a matter of choice, though it does encourage bites from larger fish. I often mix sweetcorn, luncheon meat, and casters into a mix to give it a bit of extra zing, and it usually does well. Another trick is to make a ball of groundbait and then create a little "nest" in it with your thumbs. Pour in a handful of maggots and then knead the groundbait into a ball again. The weight of the ball makes it sink quickly, and then as the ball dissolves, the maggots start to crawl out.

One last thing: don't overdo the groundbait. There may be rules relating to what you can and can't use, and some states forbid chumming altogether. Stick to the rules. Groundbait that's left on the bottom of a lake will ferment, decompose, and ulimately cause pollution. And those photos you see of catfish with huge, distended stomachs may be the result of too many protein-rich baits being chucked into the water, so go easy.

TOUCHSTONES

I was going to call this page "Fishing Heroes," but I think I know too much about people and their appetites to make that work for me any more. It's all very well idolizing Pete Rose when you're eleven years old, but it seems a bit peculiar when you get to my age. Hence "Touchstones."

What's a touchstone? Anything you want it to be, so long as it is central to your fishing life. It can be a book, a person, a memory, a smell, a bait, a favorite rod, a routine, a particular stretch of river — anything that encapsulates the angling experience.

For me it starts with the smell of a typical English fish — the roach. Very distinctive and quite unlike any other fish, this has a quality to challenge the skills of the finest perfumerie, and it makes me think of Latchmoor pond, cheese sandwiches, puncture repair kits, alleys with "No Cycling" signs, and breathless only-just-in-time-for-dinner arrivals at my parents' back door.

It goes on to *Fishing with Mr. Crabtree in All Waters*, an anthology of Bernard Venables's marvellous cartoon strip, which followed the fishing adventures of the gentle didact with the pipe and trilby hat as he taught his son Peter about fish and fishing. For thousands of boys my age, Venables's drawings were the only time we'd seen fish like barbel and carp close up, and when I close my eyes I can still see the glorious color plate of those four perch herding minnows. My copy is 40 years old and I was looking at it again just last week.

Then there's *A Passion for Angling*, a TV show I discovered by accident one night, which featured two apparent eccentrics, Chris Yates and Bob James, getting into the kind of fishing-related scrapes that wouldn't have been out of place in the books of Richmal Crompton. How staged all of this was, it's sometimes hard to tell (though some of the repartee is definitely more for the camera's benefit than a record of what actually went on), but God, how it resonated — two middle-aged men still behaving with the enthusiasm of small boys.

There's the sharp smell of the shop where we used to buy maggots on the way to the River Thames at Windsor, the sound that wicker makes as it creaks against your hip, the way a chub tugs at the rod tip, the way a landing net feels when it's freezing cold and soaking wet, looking at yourself in the mirror in a pair of long johns, wondering where the years went. There's a fishing spot as well, but I'm not telling you where that is.

The Piggery

We used to go and stay with my aunt and uncle in Scotland, where they had a small house sandwiched between a large piggery and a small burn (stream) that contained eels and trout. I caught my first brown trout here on a free-lined worm, and proudly brought it back for breakfast. I can still remember the hard, sweet smell of the piggery mixed with the aroma of grilled trout as I sat in the kitchen, smiling and eating.

THE ANGLER'S SEAT

Although many branches of the sport encourage you to get up and down the banks or go a-wading, stalk your quarry or spin for them, the archetypal image of the English angler is sat on a seat by a river. Finding the perfect seat is, therefore, something that most of us in the UK have an interest in.

I've already recounted my disastrous flirtation with a backpack/seat on page 57, so that needn't detain us here. Suffice it to say that over the years I've tried many a way to support my posterior, and I'd like to share the results with you here.

My weapons of choice: an inflatable camping cushion for the summer, and an old wicker seat basket for the winter. The inflatable cushion is one of the best pieces of angling gear I've ever owned.

First, there is unlikely to be one perfect seat that will suffice for anyone's entire angling life. As a boy, I had a superb, tiny little stool that folded ingeniously almost flat and could fit in my ancient gas-mask bag. To this day, the stool still fits in the bag, but sadly I ceased to fit on the stool long ago and now sag cartoon-style over the edges in a way that probably upsets passers-by.

PORTABILITY AND COMFORT

If you're an angler who likes to camp out in pursuit of your quarry, it's probably worth buying the most comfortable chair you can afford. Having made the decision to fish in this way, you might as well be comfortable while you're doing it. However, if you intend to move around, seek a seat that combines a carryable weight with a degree of comfort and that has legs you can adjust individually — little circular rubber stops on the feet are good, too, and prevent you from sinking too deeply into the mud.

Stadium chairs can do a job (these are the ones that open like a book and use your own body weight to maintain the correct balance and stop you from tipping backward), but the more comfortable ones are overly large for my liking. My friend Ray often makes do with a thick foam pad, and something that portable certainly has its advantages when you're working a steep bank.

For myself, I use an inflatable, rubberized cushion in summer and a small wicker seat basket in winter (with the cushion on top of it on a long day). The cushion doesn't work so well in the early mornings when there's too much dew around, but is fine into the evenings — and because of its light weight and compact size, it means I can squeeze even my inflated backside into small and awkward spots.

COMPETITIVE FISHING

While most anglers are content to pit themselves against the wiles of the fish and the vagaries of nature, for some others this isn't enough. These natural competitors need to measure their skills against those of their fellow anglers to see who comes out on top. Should you join them?

FOR

First, let's look at the benefits of competitive angling.

There's no doubt that being part of a team gives all anglers — not just beginners — a feeling of camaraderie, a sense of belonging to something that's bigger than the sum of its parts. Competitive fishing also builds team spirit and makes you aware of your responsibilities — even if they're just simple things like showing up on time, making sure you've got bait and the right tackle, and that everything's in good working order.

If you're just starting out or returning to angling after a break, there's no doubt that competitive fishing will sharpen your skills and help you to develop new ones. You'll find your casting will improve dramatically, partly because if you're fishing right, your bait won't stay in the water for very long, and partly because match fishing is usually about hitting the same spot with your bait over and over again.

You'll also become adept with many different kinds of chum or groundbait, and understand when to use the stuff that clogs together and sinks fast and when to use the stuff that bursts into an attractive cloud that entices fish into the swim without actually filling them up. You'll get faster at unhooking fish and rebaiting, you'll start to keep your disgorger behind your ear like a pencil or a cigarette, you'll become fiendishly well-organized with lots of little plastic gizmos sticking out from your seat box containing everything you need for the match so you never have to move, but can keep casting, striking, reeling in, unhooking, rebaiting, and recasting.

If you're any good, you'll win the odd cup, and you may even win a bit of prize money. You'll also find that you're part of a new fraternity, with some pretty old-fashioned values — like loyalty and reliability — along with the usual dose of infighting, cliques, and Machiavellian maneuvring. If you're consistently good — and sometimes even if you aren't — you may acquire a new nickname and a level of camaraderie not enjoyed since the schoolyard. Then there'll be the club annual general meeting to look forward to (as a match angler you'll feel compelled to attend), as well as the annual dinner and dance. As you get older you may be invited to join the committee and shape the future of the club. Angling as a social whirl, indeed . . .

AGAINST

As soon as you introduce competition to something, you change it fundamentally and forever. Take cycling. As a kid you might have biked all over the place, sometimes in a hurry, sometimes not, but usually with your head up, enjoying the mild buzz that you get with light exercise and the knowledge that you're making your own way in your own time. Competitive cycling, even at the lowest of levels, changes that experience completely. Suddenly, you're cycling not for yourself, but for the clock. Destinations become way points rather than ends in themselves, and it becomes all about the odometer and the stopwatch. It's still fun, but it's a very different kind of fun.

I'd argue that competitive fishing has the same effect. Because the pressure is on to catch fish for yourself or the team, it becomes, in effect, a race against the clock, when the smallest miscalculation in bait or depth or chumming tactics can adversely affect your final position. Some people thrive on it, but for me angling and urgency don't go together.

A ticking clock doesn't teach you patience, either. If anything it cultivates impatience, because you're always looking for the tactic that'll help you to catch immediately. It also doesn't teach you when to recognize that a particular spot is no good so you can move on, because in a match there's no moving around — you fish the spot you're given until the whistle blows. Match fishing is prescriptive. Someone else decides where you're going to fish, when you're going to start and when you're going to stop. Invariably, matches are held during the worst part of the day and they always ignore the very best times for fishing

The Fishing Match

The annual Binfield Angling Society Competition had its first and only outing on a side stretch of the river Thames. The club had two members: myself and Chick, who had recently moved to Binfield. The match lasted for five hours on the coldest day either of us could remember, and the winner weighed in with a two-ounce bleak. His reward was a pack of Passing Clouds cigarettes, purchased from the newsagents on the way back to catch the bus. The lucky winner shared the spoils with the good-humoured loser.

A year later my Uncle Jim took me to a match on the river Thame. Terribly excited, I fished well, catching roach and dace, and might even have got into the lower placings in the junior section, were it not for one mistake. The whistle blew to signify the end, I pulled the keep net out of the water and — force of habit — had a quick look at the fish before returning them to the water. No, no, no.

— dawn and dusk. Competitions thrash the water and the environment as well — all that gear trundling along the bank, all that bait and tackle pounding in, all that loose feed.

If you want to mix with like-minded anglers, join a fishing club instead. Meanwhile, just look at the phrase "competitive fishing" and think about which word comes first and which one comes second. I don't know about you, but that tells me all I need to know.

INSIDE A TROUT'S STOMACH

On the face of it, what I'm going to describe is so peculiar — and a little gross — that those anglers not familiar with the notion of looking inside a fish's stomach to see what they've been eating (and therefore what they're likely to eat next) will be appalled. Not for the first time either, probably.

There are two ways to get at what's inside a trout's stomach. The first is by using a marrow spoon, and should only ever be attempted when the fish is dead. The design is based on the long-nosed spoon used by diners to extract the tasty marrow from the inside of a long bone — this unusual shape makes it perfect for investigating Mr. Trout's stomach. Simply open the fish's mouth and insert the spoon all the way down, turning as you go. You may have to push quite hard. Shake out the contents onto a white cloth and have a magnifying glass handy to distinguish between the gunk and the invertebrates you're trying to mimic.

THE STOMACH PUMP

The second method involves using a stomach pump, and can be done when the fish is alive, rather like a bankside endoscopy. This may conjure up alarming images of large suction-powered items being forced into the gullets of tiny trout, but actually they're rather subtle devices, smaller than a syringe in most cases. Shop-bought ones are the best, and are basically a slim tube with a rubber bulb at one end. Squeeze the bulb and then gently — and the operative word is gently — insert the tube into the trout's mouth and down into its stomach. Let the rubber bulb re-inflate and it will suck in some of the contents of the trout's stomach — remove the tube and then squeeze the bulb to eject what's inside onto a white cloth. Some people reckon it's best to hold the fish upside down when you do this because it seems to keep them relatively calm.

Finally, what you find inside might not be an accurate guide to what's on the menu because fish are naturally opportunistic and will switch foods if more than one insect is hatching. It will, however, give you a better chance of making the right match on a difficult day when the fish are being persnickety. Mind you, hardcore trout anglers say that marrow spoons are for softies and that you should be able to tell what a trout's after by reading the water properly.

A marrow spoon can be used to remove the contents of a trout's stomach to see what it's been eating . . . but only when the fish is dead, of course.

CELL PHONES

Given that elsewhere I've come down firmly on the Luddite side of the fence when it comes to technology, it may surprise you to know that I'm all in favor of phones on the bankside. As long as their owners don't behave like idiots.

Rarely have I come across an item as useful to the modern angler as the cell phone. There's the simple arrangement-making side of things, of course. It ensures that dinner is on or near the table when you return, and saves it from going inside a grateful passing dog when you're running late because you hooked a double-figure catfish last cast while fishing for panfish in the margins on 3 lb. line (thus the fight took longer than normal). If you and your angling friend arrive separately, a quick phone call can set up a mutually convenient meeting point in seconds, or the pair of you can swap handy hints along the lines of "The bass have just started taking red wool on a bare hook, nothing else works, just don't ask me why." When you're fishing at distance, it's sometimes useful to swap notes over the airwaves rather than traipsing a mile up the bank only to discover your companion fast asleep under a newspaper; and that like you, he also forgot his flask and your journey has been in vain.

A modern cell phone should include a digital camera — two megapixels is adequate for snaps in good light — which not only saves you having to bring a camera, but also allows you to taunt angling friends at work with photographs of your catch. You can even use the video-capture feature to grab a short clip of the final moments of the fight — though, of course, you should never let a Hollywood moment get in the way of landing a fish properly and carefully.

My car key seconds after the end fell off. Thanks to a cell phone, Ray was on his way in minutes, bringing me a spare.

Phones are also useful in emergencies — for example, if one were idiotic enough to break one's car key in the middle of nowhere in the middle of the night.

Apart from that, knock yourself out. Either make sure the phone is switched to vibrate for the convenience of other anglers, or avail yourself of a nice, subtle ring tone — a bit of George Gershwin or Aaron Copland, perhaps.

Alternatively, I read of someone who spent time recording the sounds made by classic reels spinning in the Hardy Museum in Northumberland, England, and now sells them as ring tones that you can download from the Internet (www.salmonreel.com). If that's not calming enough, the same site sells the sounds of goats, woodpeckers, and a swan trumpeting.

TRADITIONAL TACKLE

For some, using traditional tackle is something to be pursued with an almost religious fervor. Not only do they love their cane rods, centerpins, and battered old creels, but some of them dress up in plus-fours and Sherlock Holmes hats. Stark, staring, raving mad, I tell you.

I blame Chris Yates and *A Passion For Angling* (see page 96). All that wicker, tea, and bicycles have turned the head of many a simple angler, including, it must be said, me.

An old-fashioned centerpin is a joy to use, especially on a river.

I've always admired traditional tackle. When I started fishing it was at the beginning of fiberglass, which, thanks to its winning characteristics of strength, lightness, and value for money, was sweeping all before it. In the early days I still came across the odd cane rod (and once an enormous roach pole that could easily have doubled as a mast for the America's Cup), but they were either battered old things used by old men or varnished, expensive beauties in shop windows, far beyond the reach of my meagre pockets. I persisted with a centerpin in my early days out of poverty rather than any affinity, and made the switch to a spinning reel as soon as I was able. Indeed, it would not be for another 25 years that I felt flush enough to dip a toe into the world of traditional tackle and buy a second-hand cane rod — just for fun.

And what fun. My friend Sean reckoned he had a cane rod that was so flexible, he could bend it in a complete circle, and would do so occasionally, offering it as

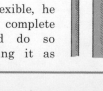

something for me to jump through, perhaps. Taking mine carefully from its tattered bag and popping it together, I could see what he meant. I gave it a cautious waggle up and down, and the thing started wobbling back and forth with a weird, sinuous grace. It's hard to describe. I've got great carbon-fiber rods, but when you whip them back and forth it's like watching a mathematical equation in action. With a cane rod, it's an animal weaving this way and that. (This preparatory whip back and forth has become something of a tradition for me before attaching the reel; once, the top section of the rod flew off and I had the mortifying task of knocking on a nice lady's door and asking if I could have my rod back).

I'd bought a centerpin reel from the same chap — a cheap Leeds model, remaindered when a tackle shop had shut — and used it intermittently. Putting these two old-timers together and then fishing for tench and crucian carp showed me what

Cane rods are every bit as efficient as their modern carbon-fiber counterparts — more fun, too.

I'd been missing. I wouldn't like to hook a carp or a pike on one, but for fish up to 5 lb. or so, the 'pin is a revelation. You don't realize how the fixed-spool technology acts as a buffer between you and the fight; with the 'pin, it's a direct line between you and the fish. Throw in a rod that's bent in an often hilarious hoop, and it's hard not to laugh out loud sometimes.

Of course, now I've got a creel (hand-made in Somerset willow, and embarrassingly expensive), a wicker seat basket (a bargain), and the odd perch float from a garage sale. I can't justify adding anything more to the "collection," but I will if I see a bargain. Traditional tackle is worth a lot of money these days and, as an investment, is likely to keep going up year on year. Fortunately, the same can't be said for the aforementioned antique clothing, which looks as bad today as it did back then.

My wicker seat basket — with its distinctive letterbox opening in the top.

That's Not a Fish

And after all that antique elegance, let's be having an abbreviated list of some of the things that anglers have caught down the years that turned out not be fish after all, including:

Other peoples' tackle, used condoms full of water (which 'fight' like enormous bream), tricycles (but never bicycles), denim shorts, clerical collars, terrapins, your younger brother, blinds, the ankles of the lady who was walking behind you, a sorry sack of dead kittens, bats, a pair of handcuffs, a mannequin, assorted coots, ducks, and swans, a handbag with shoes inside weighed down with stones, brassieres, dead fish (which seem to be able to attach themselves at will to a static bait and then die all over again), sanitary towels, sheep, a passing motorbike, shopping carts, socks, scissors, another entire rod and reel (but fortunately no angler), rope, lots of rope, mussels, top hats, crayfish, rubber boots, paperback books, a full bottle of wine, the bonnet of a car, Muppets (there's something disturbing about catching Kermit), an acoustic guitar, stair carpet, LPs, a Halloween mask, a tin of biscuits, and a dartboard.

Amazing that there's room for any fish in there, really . . .

UNUSUAL TECHNIQUES

These days many anglers turn to technology to provide the answer to a particular fishing problem, but with a little thought you can often come up a solution that works just as well, but doesn't cost anything. Anglers have always been ingenious and innovative, and here are just a few of the unusual ideas I've collected and tried out down the years with considerable success.

I'm going to be completely honest and steal my first one from Mr. Crabtree. It solves the problem of how to keep surface-feeding fish in your area long enough to catch them. The problem with loose-feeding on the surface is that the wind and currents will simply take the bait away, and if you've been canny in your choices, the fish will surely follow. So you don't want to do that. Instead, plumb the depth. Then, take a slice of bread that's been baked hard and poke a hole through the middle. Tie string line round it and then tie a stone to the other end of the string — obviously the point is that the distance between the bread and the stone equals the depth of your intended location. Lob the lot out into the water. The stone will act as an anchor to keep the bread in place, thus helping to concentrate the attentions of any surface-feeding fish. I use string instead of line because it degrades in the water more quickly after use.

If you've got a particularly shy fish in your sights, it may well be put off by too much — or the wrong kind of — terminal tackle. Reduce the odds of rejection by free-lining (just using the bait and the hook, see page 124) or using some natural material as a float. If you're fishing a river, tie a bit of stick to your line, drop the bait in by your feet and let it float down with the rest of the river junk to where the fish are lying in wait. Don't just watch the stick for bites, though; instead, watch and feel the line as if you were touch ledgering.

LONG-DISTANCE BAITING

If you need to fish at a greater distance than you can cast and there's a decent wind, consider using a balloon to drift your bait across the lake. Blow up the balloon and attach it to the line with a paperclip. Then drop the bait-and-balloon rig into the water at your feet and let the wind carry it over the lake. This method will take a bait much farther than most of us can cast. When it reaches the required spot, strike smartly to separate the balloon from the line (remember, it's

Use a balloon attached to the line to carry your bait across large distances, then strike to free the balloon and sink the bait.

only held on with a paperclip), and the bait will sink to the bottom. There are two disadvantages to this method — first, you can only fish in the direction that the wind is blowing; and second, you must go round afterward and collect up the balloons that have blown to shore on the other side of the lake. It's very important that you don't leave them behind because they're a real hazard to wildlife.

PVA bags slowly dissolve on contact with water and are an effective way to enclose both bait and hook

SMALL SPACES

We all know that fish love to patrol the shelves and margins of a lake, but too often they seem to favor the opposite bank or the islands in the middle, away from all those anglers trying to be quiet. However, unless you're a bit of an expert, it's quite hard to cast accurately into a small strip of water and you usually end up too far out from the opposite bank, or tangled up in the bushes above it. One trick I've used successfully involves two stages. First, you need to identify a section of the far bank that isn't covered in dense bushes or trees, then you need to use a large, smooth bait with none of the hook sticking out. Overcast — deliberately land your bait on the opposite bank — and then gently draw it back into the water. If you want to fish a bait that doesn't cover the hook, put the lot inside a PVA bag (the kind that dissolves in water). That way it shouldn't catch on anything. Works for me.

Finally, fly fishermen are used to catching small trout out of tiny streams but you'd be surprised at the other fish you can catch from water that barely seems able to cover their backs. Plenty of fish grow fat in small streams, where there's less competition and predators are few and far between. It's also a great learning experience for the angler, as small streams tend to be clearer and thus require more careful approach work, more accurate casting, quieter feet and so on. I use a short rod — even down to 7 feet (2.1 m.) when necessary — and fish and move, spending only ten minutes or so in each spot before moving on. Bait is normally a single worm free-lined on a medium-sized hook, trundled along the bottom with a couple of shot squeezed on the line, or dropped on its own into a weed bed.

Ignore small streams at your peril — they often hold surprisingly large fish.

BEAUTIES AND BEASTS

I'm not the kind of angler who's part naturalist, or half marine biologist, or even one-quarter herbalist, and I'm slightly in awe of those who are. You know the type: the ones who can tell one bird from another by its song, who know not just the half-dozen obvious trees and plants (willow, stinging nettle), and whose knowledge of animals and their habits extends beyond basic need-to-know information along the lines of "Look out — cowpat."

So I have some sympathy when people passing by ask what kind of a fish I've caught, or even if another angler comes frowning up to me carrying something and asks for advice. ("It's a grayling, and no, I don't know why it's in a lake. Owner thought it was a good idea?") But I do know my fish, and over the years have formed strong opinions as to their relative aesthetic natures, such that I feel comfortable in presenting you with my top five most beautiful European fish, followed by the top five plug-uglies.

THE BEAUTIES
In reverse order, these are:

✦ I'm going to stick my neck out here and put the barbel in fifth place. Yes, there's intelligence in those eyes, but it's a sort of unpredictable canine cunning and there are those weird barbules hanging down from its mouth that spider their way along the bottom of the river looking for food and give it that creepy I'm-going-to-feel-my-way-all-over-your-fingers-while-you're-asleep look.

✦ Perch, like bass, are fantastic-looking in principle, but they're never quite the right size. Under a pound and they've got no definition; anything bigger and they look like they've spent too much time in the gym — massive shoulders, wide eyes, in-your-face dorsals. And, of course, those I-can-swallow-my-own-body mouths . . .
✦ Crucian carp are pretty but dumb. They're fakers, like gold plate.
✦ The dace comes close. It's got the same general fishy-footprint as a trout, it's got the feel of a roach, but it actually wants to be a chub. When small it has the characteristics of a classic silver fish, but the larger it gets the more chub-like it becomes, with its fins picking up color and back broadening.
✦ But the winner is . . . the rainbow trout. A touchstone fish for millions of anglers the world over. Beautiful coloring whether it's large or small, smart, aggressive and always a joy to catch.

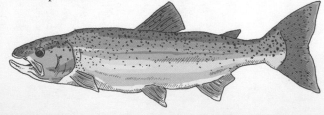

The rainbow trout is a fish loved by anglers the world over, and my reigning pin-up fish.

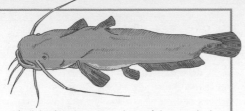

Of all the fish that swim, the catfish is surely the hardest hit by the ugly stick.

THE BOOBIES

+ In fifth place, the bleak. Ugly, good-for-nothing fish that swarm around baits meant for daintier fish like schoolboys around a football.
+ Perhaps surprisingly, next comes the rudd. There's something not quite right here — too golden, too red, like a fish from Chernobyl. And any mouth that curves up like that is not to be trusted.
+ Next up, the eel. Oh, where to start? With the zombie eyes, the slime, or the impossible-to-keep-hold-of writhing? Doesn't feature higher up the list only because large specimens are strangely beautiful.
+ In second place, the zander. A controversial choice, perhaps, given how much they resemble the beloved American walleye. Nevertheless, zander look like two other fish that have been sawn in half and then stuck together again for a joke. And they have the mad eyes of an eel.
+ But, at number one with a bullet, it has to be the catfish. Ugly beyond belief, revered only for their size, seemingly without any bones, looking like a cross between a giant slug that someone's stepped on and something out of John Carpenter's *The Thing*.

Barbless Hooks

Looking back, I can't actually remember the last time I used a barbed hook, but I'm sure that there hasn't been a place for one in my tackle box for years. I was a reluctant convert and remained convinced that barbed hooks had an extra stickability until both my fishing clubs banned them as part of their rules — no exceptions.

Now I can't imagine going back to barbs. They catch on everything — clothing, trees, bushes, me — and are ten times harder to get out of whatever they're hooked into. They also damage a fish's mouth in a way that barbless hooks do not. Of course, they're both puncture wounds, but by their very nature barbs are harder to get out, especially when a fish is hooked deep in the throat and you have to remove the hook mostly by feel alone.

Those anglers who argue that it's easier to keep a fish on the line when you're using a barbed hook are plain wrong. In years of using barbless hooks, I've lost many fish to my own stupidity, but I've yet to lose one because of a barbless hook. They're an unnecessary unkindness, and even lures that are still sold with barbed hooks should have them squeezed to nothing with a pair of pliers.

MAKE A WORMERY

Worms are associated with fishing for good reason — they're an excellent bait and will catch virtually anything that swims, large or small. They're expensive to buy, though, and don't last very long, so what about growing your own? It's easy with this simple-to-make wormery.

The best housing for this is an old plastic garbage can, because it'll give you the structure for your wormery without you having to actually build anything. Make some holes round the bin about 2 inches (5 cm.) up from the bottom, about 8 inches (20 cm.) apart; this is for drainage. Then do the same around the top of the can. Pour in about 6 inches (15 cm.) worth of sand and/or gravel, and then on top of that put a sheet of polythene with holes drilled for drainage. Next, add about another 8 inches (20 cm.) of compost/leaf mold/bedding material.

How to get the worms? Well, you need about 100 to start a wormery of this size properly, so you can buy them, gather them from a good compost heap, or collect them for yourself. A good way to do the latter is to put a large square of carpet down on the soil for 24 hours or sprinkle a mixture of dish-washing liquid and warm water on the ground to bring them up to the surface.

Once you've added your worms, tip a couple of handfuls of kitchen scraps into the can, and finish off with a few handfuls of wet torn-up newspaper. Pop the lid back on and leave it for a couple of weeks.

Although worms will thrive on most things, they're not so keen on meat, fish, or citrus fruit. Instead, feed them a varied diet of kitchen scraps, weeds, leaves, grass cuttings, and other waste from the garden that you'd normally take to the dump. Don't overfeed, though — wait until they're obviously turning the contents of the bin into compost before you add more food. If the wormery starts to smell, it's too wet and you'll need to add some more shop-bought compost to soak up the excess. A wormery like this will make a good home for nightcrawlers, brandlings, or dendrabenas, as long as you keep the lid on until it's time to wrangle your worms. I get mine on the morning of the fishing trip. It's a sort of ritual to go outside with a cup of coffee and a bait box and slowly work your fingers through the gunk to collect enough worms for the trip. Lovely.

Whether you buy a wormery or make your own, having a constant supply or fresh worms throughout the year will save you money and catch you fish.

WE DON'T DO THAT ANY MORE

It's funny how times change, how the methods adopted by one generation with scarcely a second thought come to be viewed as eccentric at best or cruel at worst. Angling has changed over the years, and although some of those changes sit uncomfortably with me, there are certain things I'm happy to see the back of.

If the man I am today went fishing for pike with the boy I used to be, there would be — to say the least — a clash of cultures.

As a boy, it never occurred to me not to fish for pike with a live bait. Never again.

The boy has saved his pocket money so he can buy the legendary Jardine snap tackle, a device so bound up with pike fishing and so resonant that even today the name gives him a frisson of excitement. Sold in a little brown paper bag, the snap tackle comprises two sets of barbed treble hooks on a stiff metal trace. A roach is quickly caught on a piece of bread paste; one hook goes into the back of the fish just below the dorsal, and the other into the top lip. The whole thing is then suspended underneath a paint-peeled pike bobber and hurled out into the middle of the pond to await a run.

It doesn't take long. Neither does the fight, because the pike in this pond are jacks — baby pike — that rarely top 3 lb. As the boy reels in, the man beside him notices that there's no landing net and is about to offer his own when the boy reaches down and pulls a curious looking object out of the reeds where it's lain hidden. Later he'll tell the man how he made it in metalwork at school — an old javelin sawn in half, a thread bored into one end and then a large pirate's hook, bent and sharpened in the school forge, screwed into the top. It's a gaff, and as the pike is dragged to shore the boy expertly inserts the point of the hook into the soft part of the pike's mouth, under the chin and behind the jawbone. Human mouths are arranged in the same way.

On the bank, unhooking takes longer than expected because one of the treble hooks is way down the throat and the pike won't stop thrashing about. Eventually it comes out and the pike is dropped into the keep net, where it sinks to the bottom and sulks.

The man watches all this, appalled.

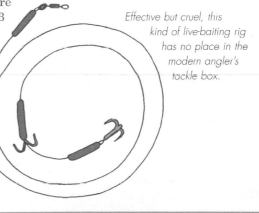

Effective but cruel, this kind of live-baiting rig has no place in the modern angler's tackle box.

🐟 FISHING LITERATURE

The definition of what makes a good fishing book depends entirely on what you're hoping to get out of it. If all you require is for angling to be reduced to a set of step-by-step instructions that tell you how to do something, then you've got more great literature than you can shake a rod rest at. Personally, I prefer something with a bit more soul, like the books mentioned here, but it's worth spending some time finding your own favorites.

Even the best angling book is a poor substitute for the real thing, but down the years I've assembled a decent library of books (helped in no small part by my brother, who has embraced Internet shopping with considerable enthusiasm), and I offer a few of them here, in chronological order of publication, for the next time you're in a second-hand bookstore — local or online.

An Open Creel by H.T. Sheringham (1910). A delightful ramble through many different styles of fishing. It disguises the many hints and tips with a narrative that's both deft and descriptive. Funny, too: "My dear fellow, for sheer unadulterated vileness, last Saturday stands in a class by itself. Why to begin with . . ."

Roach Fishing by 'Faddist' (1936). Much of the basic material had already appeared elsewhere in different publications such as *The Field, The Fishing Gazette, Game and Gun*, but I include it here as a fine example of the early art of specimen hunting, where an angler concentrates on a single species at the expense of all others. It's also full of astute observations to strike a chill into the heart of any angler: "In other words, roach are at their best when the weather is at its worst."

My River by Wilfred Gavin Brown (1947). A highly anecdotal account that goes far beyond a single river — or fishing, really — summed up by the beautiful account of a first fish followed by the girl of 16 who offered the author a bright red apple while her grandmother scowled at him through the window of their cottage. Someone knows their fairy tales.

Fishing with Mr. Crabtree in All Waters by Bernard Venables (1964). While I never understood all the sea-fishing stuff at the beginning, the cartoons depicting Mr Crabtree and his son Peter in their always-successful quest for various freshwater fish are evocative and entertaining. I learned a lot from them, too.

Freshwater Fishing by Fred Buller and Hugh Falkus (1975). For an all-round grounding in freshwater fish and fishing, you won't go far wrong with this. It's encyclopedic, entirely black and white, and reads a bit like it was written by a pair of slightly grumpy physics teachers. But, by gum, they know their stuff, and you'll find more useful information in here than in ten years' worth of fishing magazines.

Casting at the Sun by Christopher Yates (1986). Yates is a rarity — an angling writer who knows how to write — and this "study of a near psychotic obsession" chronicles the adventures of the inveterate carp chaser. Yates's books are always worth seeking out.

I Remember: Reflections on Fishing in Childhood compiled by Joe Cowley (1995). A fabulous compendium featuring contributions from Bernard Venables, Frederick Forsyth, George Melly, Peter Stone, Barrie Rickards, Nick Fisher, and Bernard Cribbins among others. Varied, and makes a good present, too.

For those times when you can't go fishing, a good book is a respectable alternative — and a very good one can be revisited time and again.

Hooked by Fen Montaigne (1998). Ostensibly the story of a fly-fishing trip across the Russian Federation, this is much more: a character study of a people adrift in the post-Communist regime ("not so much a road as a direction") and an indictment of the obsessive race toward an all-out Hollywood-style capitalism, set against a backdrop of potato patches from the White Sea to the Pacific Ocean.

Trout at Ten Thousand Feet by John Bailey (2001). I'm not a great fan of exotic fishing trips and the stories related to them, but this is different. Bailey observes: "You'd think that air travel, e-mails, satellite phones, and the rest would have robbed the world of her secrets. You'd be wrong." This is book is a descriptive joy, thoughtful, reflective, and funny.

In recommending these books, I'm painfully aware of the ones left out. Geoffrey Bucknall's *Fishing Days* springs to mind as a book I loved as a boy, Dick Walker's *Still Water Angling* is a mine of information of the best kind, while books by "BB" (aka Denys Watkins Pitchford) and Arthur Ransome paint delightful pictures of simpler times, when the fish mattered more than the fishing tackle you caught them on. Finally, of all the magazines on the market, I'd recommend *Waterlog*, co-founded by Chris Yates and full of the oddest, most interesting angling stories around. It's subscription only, but you can find more information by visiting the web site (www.waterlogmagazine.co.uk).

FISHING WITH THE FAMILY

There comes a point in every angler's life when they are foolishly tempted to try to include their nearest and dearest in the sport that so consumes them. This is fraught with difficulties, and requires strategy and careful planning if it's not to end in complete disaster.

Those anglers who are single and fancy-free can move on from here — you may be temporarily unlucky in love, but your angling life has a clarity and simplicity that the rest of us can only dream of. For the remainder who have family of one sort or another to consider, best to lay your plans carefully.

Choose good weather. No spouse or partner is going to have their head turned away from the dark side if you force them to sit next to you under your umbrella in the teeth of a fierce storm. Remember, they're probably not going to have any adequate outdoor gear, so go in the summer and make it a pleasant, balmy afternoon. You can even take a picnic with a bottle of wine (for them, not you).

Choose somewhere easy — easy to get to by car or public transport, and then easy to get to the waterside once you arrive. Ensure there are no natural obstacles either, because people find it hard to see the fun in high-stepping at speed through long wet grass holding a baby under one arm and a picnic basket in the other, while being pursued by a herd of cows.

Choose a place where you stand a good chance of catching a decent-sized fish — snatching tiddlers all afternoon might do wonders for your competitive edge, but is only likely to confirm your partner's prejudices that catching lots of tiny things is a peculiar pastime for another grown-up. A 5 lb. bass, on the other hand, really looks like a fish, and presented in the right way can appear almost beautiful.

Your partner can bring their own entertainment, but try to dissuade them from getting iPodded up. You want to engage their senses in the world around them, not let them cut themselves off.

Don't push your luck. Pack up early so that you can share the sunset together and talk about the day. And don't be disappointed if at the end of the trip they still don't "get it." Only the stoniest-hearted partner won't appreciate the effort you've made, and they should refrain from giving you any earache for a few months. Indeed, it will allow you to lay plans for stage two: the holiday in the Bahamas . . . with perhaps a bit of bone fishing thrown in.

Some members of the family will undoubtedly enjoy going fishing with you more than others. Better take a tin hat.

THE LITTLE FISH

Your life's angling adventure often starts with a net on a bamboo stick
And little fish — lots of them. That's how mine began.

Keith and I — the summer before he announced that he was to be called "Chick" — used to cycle down to the other side of the village where there was a long, deep stretch of river followed by a weir, followed by rapids, followed by a wonderful run with huge weed beds and gravel straights. We'd dump the bikes, strip off shoes and socks (we were in short trousers, of course) and wade in, shoving the nets into the weed beds like lunatics and inspecting the contents with greedy eyes.

We netted sticklebacks, minnows, and bullheads, and marvelled at these monsters in miniature and how — even at that tiny size — their flanks shimmered in the sun; not the bullhead, of course. He remained a stoic muddy brown. We caught them, but they captivated us, and when Keith-who-was-to-become-Chick scooped his net into the long weed bed halfway down the run and came up with a little trout, that was the start. From then on, we were both anglers. Years later I remember fishing a famous stretch of the river Stour for barbel on a miserable, freezing day. Last cast I caught a minnow, and just for a second . . .

As you angle, remember the little fish, because they make boys — or girls — again out of us all.

CRITTERS THAT BITE

When you go fishing, you discover quickly that fish aren't the only hungry
creatures you're likely to meet. If, like me, you attract mosquitoes and large
biting flies like the proverbial steaming pile of ordure, you need to take steps
to sort it out. And it's best not to muck about.

Though I'm normally a fan of natural remedies, I've found that gentle infusions like citronella and eucalyptus are unable to persuade insects to bug off, and these days I opt for industrial-strength DEET-based repellents. These have their own drawbacks. Anything above 50% concentration can irritate your skin, and you need to keep it away from your eyes and mouth. Similarly, you should try to keep the ends of your fingers clear of repellent because it'll rub off on the bait and fish hate it.

Although some people use a pump spray for application, I prefer a stick because it's generally easier to use and a lot less messy. In really bad conditions (where there are a lot of sandflies, for example), I'll wear a hat with a no-see-em net in the brim that I can roll down if necessary. It interferes with your vision a bit, but it's better than getting bitten to pieces.

Of course, by far the most effective repellent is a cigarette, a cigar, or a smelly pipe, but those days are far behind us now.

NON-STOP FISHING

Given the access-all-areas, open-all-hours nature of modern life, it's hardly surprising that some anglers object when other people tell them exactly when they can and can't fish. They need — as the modern vernacular puts it — to get over themselves.

In the 21st century, waiting is, it seems, a bad thing. Thus, stores are open 24/7, television runs throughout the night, wildly expensive items can be bought on credit and enjoyed immediately (naturally, only homeowners need apply — the rest of us don't have anything the lenders want), and many anglers now want fishing to be on tap whenever they're in the mood for it.

Now I don't want to drag angling back into the dark ages, and I certainly don't yearn for some idealized version of the 1950s when — frankly — things were a bit crap, but everyone needs to take a break. Fish need it, not just to spawn but to lose their fear of man, for their fishy hearts to beat again to the rhythms of the river and the lake, away from temptation and the siren song of the spinner, jig, feeder, or ball of groundbait.

The waters need it, too. Their banks need time to recover, their approaches need a rest from anglers' boots, and lanes, trails — even parking lots — deserve a break. And so does the rest of the natural world, unless we want every water we fish to be a blank, man-made puddle where anglers can fish from their cars, eat hot sandwiches from the on-site café, and catch stocked fish cast after cast to a soundtrack of bite alarms and iPods.

Some people argue that their lives are so busy they can't squeeze in any fishing unless it's available all-year round. Crap. Watch less television, don't go to the

Give yourself and the fish a break from time to time — you'll return to angling refreshed.

bar so often, get up a couple of hours earlier, and fish somewhere local rather than driving for hours to fish somewhere that's got a good reputation.

Lack of time isn't the real reason people want to fish all-year round; it's because nobody waits for anything any more, and that archetypal angling virtue — patience — has apparently run out. I think it's a shame. As a cold beer after a long, hard day tastes better than the one you drink at 11 in the morning just because the bars are open and you can, so the first cast on the opening day of the season is so much sweeter because you've spent the previous three months dreaming about it. Restraint brings its own reward.

THE "TRASH" FISH

Rarely has one breed of fish been so revered by some and despised by others. What on earth did the carp do to anglers to deserve such wildly inconsistent treatment? There must be some ghastly skeletons in its fishy closet.

Consider these quotations:

"The weight was intensely satisfying and the beauty of the thing I'd caught made me burst into song." Chris Yates, *The Deepening Pool.*

"You just toss it back there on the bank behind you, son. It's a piece of junk." Unnamed Texan angler to his son.

It's hard to believe they're talking about the same fish, but they are. For better or worse, the carp provokes strong feelings among anglers, and above all others is the fish you either love or hate.

Those who love carp champion its cunning, size (and resulting brute power), and longevity. There's something special, they argue, about trying to catch a fish that could be more than 40 years old and thus in many cases older than the angler pursuing it. Certainly carp had a reputation for years of being so difficult to catch that many anglers refused even to try for them so as to avoid being humiliated, and it wasn't really until the '50s that carp fishing became practical and desirable. Since then it's grown to become the most important style of coarse fishing in the western world.

Carp can thrive in waters where the pollution will cause other fish to struggle — and American anglers are coming to understand their appeal.

TAKE OUT THE TRASH

Outside of the US, that is. In England, where carp — even quite large carp — are derided as "trash fish" and tossed aside, the contrast couldn't be more profound. This disdain seems to be based partly on a belief that carp are no good to eat, partly on general prejudice against non-indigenous species, and partly on a conviction that carp feed so hard and grow so fast that they muscle aside all the other species in a particular water — something that infuriates anglers who pursue fish like trout and bass. However, the carp isn't a bad neighbor, it's just a better survivor than most other freshwater fish, and if over time carp are showing more than bass in a water, it's usually because there's a deeper problem, like pollution or low levels of oxygen.

In the end, this may be its salvation. Many urban rivers are too polluted to support the more popular North American sport fish, but carp are hanging in there. That means the first fish many American kids catch is going to be a carp. And we all know how much that first fish resonates through an angler's life, informing and influencing what they choose to fish for later on. The carp may yet win over the doubters.

CARING FOR FISH

For those who are anti-fishing, the thought that anglers actually care for the fish they catch is a peculiar does-not-compute notion. True, most of us could do better, and there are certainly some branches of the sport that lag behind others, but in the end it's one angler and one fish at a time, and if you treat them well, the fish and the sport will thrive.

Anglers sometimes talk about a "connection" to fish and fishing. For some, it's a boyhood thing, a way to recapture the carefree days of kid-dom when things were easier and less complicated; for others, it's more to do with the ancient hunting instinct — catching fish for food and all that. Whichever theory you subscribe to, it's clear that alongside that connection comes a responsibility to care for the individual fish you catch and the fish population as a whole.

INDIVIDUAL CARE

The biggest single attribute you can bring to a fish is confidence when you handle it. If you grab at a fish or hold it too loosely or too tightly, it'll either flip out of your hands and onto the bank or you'll damage its scales. You should also try the following:

+ Don't bully the fish in too quickly. If it's still got plenty of fight in it when you get it to the bank, then it's more likely to hurt itself by flapping about.
+ If in doubt, use your landing net rather than swinging the fish in — if it falls off and smacks into the bank (or the water) it can do a lot of damage.

+ If you're unhooking a small fish in your hands, keep a light tension on the line and simply circle the fish with your hand to keep it in place while you remove the hook.
+ Don't chuck fish back into the water, even if they're small, because it can concuss them.
+ If you're wading, or the fish is of a comfortable size, you may be able to unhook it without taking it out of the water at all.
+ For larger fish, if you can't unhook them in the water, use an unhooking mat on a flat surface, or at least move them away from the water's edge and onto soft ground.
+ Once the fish is in the net, put the rod in its rest and set the reel so that line can run off it freely — this ensures the hook doesn't get jerked when you carry the fish up the bank in the net.
+ Keep them in the net for unhooking. With large fish, I find that covering their head with a part of the net helps to keep them calm.

For large fish, an unhooking mat is a must as it protects them from being damaged by rough ground.

Always wet your hands a little in the water before handling a fish or taking it from the net

- If you have to remove them from the net for unhooking, hold them in a damp cloth and always wet your hands before handling them.
- Some anglers dab a little specially formulated antiseptic around the area where the hook has gone in — your tackle shop can advise you about this.
- If you're going to be photographing your fish, turn to page 61.
- If you've caught a large fish from a river, don't just slip it back in. Instead, hold it loosely in your hands with its head pointing upstream until it has the strength to swim away on its own.

COMMUNITY CARE

As an angler, you not only have a duty of care to the fish that you catch, but you should also consider our fishy brothers and sisters in a much broader sense. Here are some steps you can take to care for fish as a whole:

- Observe the rules of each water that you fish regarding banned methods and banned baits. If you disagree, get involved and let someone know, rather than just ignoring the rules.
- Pay special attention to those rules regarding keep-net dipping (this prevents disease from spreading water-by-water courtesy of visiting anglers' keep nets). Better still, don't use a keep net at all.

- Don't move fish from one water to another — for example, by catching a small fish from a river to use as bait in a lake 20 miles away. This is a good way to spread disease.
- Research and then join a fishing club that demonstrates a responsible, long-term approach to the waters it looks after — rather than just filling them full of tiddlers.
- Take an active role in any fishing club you join, working from the inside to make changes for the better.
- When you go fishing, take a cell phone with you and have numbers on it so you can report pollution or dangerous animals straight away.
- Join a conservation society or other organization that uses common law to make polluters pay for the mess they make in our rivers and lakes. It is well worth your money. It helps angling clubs, too.
- Make sure that you have the correct fishing license, that it's up to date, and that you have the stamps you need for any regulated species. At least some of the license money goes back into water management, which is a good thing. Anyway, whether you want to support these efforts or not, having a license is the law.

Looking after fish should be a pleasure as well as a duty, an investment in angling's future rather than a chore. We owe it to ourselves and those who follow to care for all the fish we catch and for all the ones we'll never see.

CATCH MORE, CATCH FASTER

For a new breed of angler, enough is never quite enough. First they want to catch a fish every time they go fishing, then they want to catch a double-figure fish, then they want the biggest fish in the lake, then the biggest fish in the country, then the biggest fish in someone else's country. And so it goes on.

There's a very pretty song by Peter Yarrow, an American folksinger who was in the trio Peter, Paul, and Mary. It's called *That's Enough For Me* and it's a gentle summary of an ordinary life, led well, but, in the eyes of some, perhaps unremarkably. It's a sentiment that too many modern anglers could never be accused of sharing.

I'm not sure where it came from. A general impatience, perhaps, certainly a lack of grace, and a diminishing understanding of what lies at the deep heart of fishing, have all brought us to a place where the only questions being asked are "How big?" and "How many?" This has become an article of faith for many modern British anglers, who would rather watch television than have their time wasted by a passing tench or bream snaffling the bait laid so carefully for a large carp. Indeed, tucked up in their tents many do watch TV, or at least a portable DVD player. Thus, an expensive weekend spent pursuing a large carp is considered wasted if all that comes to the bank are a handful of smaller models or, perish the thought, nothing at all.

This attitude casts fishing as a competition, even when there's nobody else competing. As a result, anglers measure themselves against other anglers' records, or whatever protein-bait-stuffed porker is weighing down the front page of a fishing newspaper or magazine, or bulging out of the screen from a Web site that week.

Yes, this fish actually appears larger than the angler — often no mean feat.

FACTORY FISHING

Angling magazines fan the flames, encouraging readers to buy the latest tackle and baits, implying that if they don't, they'll never be able to rack up a score like their colleagues'. Fishing becomes like shopping, where a successful trip is judged first by the labels on the bags and then by how full they are.

Manufacturers respond to — and add to — this culture with ever more expensive and technical "innovations," which we wiser heads know are usually better at catching anglers than they are fish. It's an embarrassing business walking into the tackle shop and knowing that your choice is between the new 12-foot Predator or the 13-foot Super Specialist, since I am neither a proper predator nor very special at anything. But then, like camouflage clothing, I suppose this is designed to attract the soldier angler, the one who classes himself as a hunter, and not one of us "wimps" with our Thermoses of coffee and funny hats.

I understand why. There's an unholy, unspoken pact between publishers and advertisers, whereby both feed off the still-breathing corpse of the angling public by cross-promoting their products and services, articles and competitions, give-aways and freebies. It's not subtle and not really deceitful because it's so in-your-face, but it supports this culture of the instant hit — angling as crack cocaine, if you like — promoting the notion that anyone who doesn't sign up doesn't get it, is missing out on the real thing because they're not catching more or catching faster.

Seeking It Elsewhere

It drives people abroad, this lust for the instant hit. Suddenly carp in the UK aren't big enough, not when there are real net-busters just over the channel in France, or further south where the Ebro catfish are so huge that you use carp as live bait to catch them.

Best of all, there are plenty of folk on hand to make sure you need never interact with the country you're visiting, so you can get a good English breakfast, a few beers, then drive out to the water where your swim's been pre-baited with sexy chemical particles and is now filled with fish so obliging that they'll swim up to the shore and tickle your toes.

(What's truly funny is when these package-holiday anglers decide they're ready for a real adventure and go, let us say, taimen fishing in Mongolia, expecting the same sort of deal, but end up getting chased by bears and catching nothing but a sore butt.)

There's always been more to going fishing than catching fish. It's about reconnecting with the world outside the living room and the office and the TV and the computer screen; it's about re-acquainting yourself with pouring rain and freezing winds; it's about catching loads and having a laugh; and it's about not catching anything and still feeling good about it. The world's a fast enough and competitive enough place without anglers joining in, because as soon as we do, as soon as we fall for all that nonsense, we become consumers of fish and of fishing. And in the end, that diminishes us and everything that angling stands for. It will be our ruin.

Full nets and empty heads: don't judge the success of a fishing trip solely by the number of fish you catch; the true angling experience is at once more rewarding and more subtle.

🐟 FISHING AND CAMPING

By this I don't mean going off with your pals on a camping trip that happens to include a bit of fishing. I mean camping out while you fish through the night for large specimens — usually carp, pike, eels, or catfish — relying on electronic alarms to tell you when you've got a bite.

Temperamentally, I ought to love the style of fishing that sets you up in a little one-person tent with a snazzy bed chair, sleeping bag, stove, and lots of the other bits and pieces, because I love camping so much. So how come I've never done it?

For those unfamiliar with the concept, it goes like this. Large fish become large by being crafty and difficult to catch. Thus, anglers who wish to catch them must demonstrate enormous patience while waiting for these superior, shy, and highly developed monsters to be fooled into taking the bait. Fortunately, resourceful anglers have developed a style of fishing that enables them to do exactly that, thus demonstrating their almost preternatural powers of patience. They turn up, tackle up, bait up, cast out, and then go to sleep.

These bivouac anglers seem to have forgotten one or more essential items . . .

You may have seen evidence of these curious nocturnal folk on waters all over the country, identifiable by their distinctive little tents — like green domes — that hug the water's edge and often emit smoke signals or a terrifying snoring sound.

Many anglers stay more than one night and fish more than one rod, using a system of colored lights or different sounds to help them distinguish which of their rods is the one with the bite. Imagine how utterly disorientating it must be to be yanked out of sleep like that, probably full of coffee and reconstituted beef stew, warm one second and stumbling around on frozen feet the next. It's a wonder they don't fall in.

On many waters around the UK, this is the only acceptable face of night fishing. Certainly all the clubs I've ever belonged to have banned the use of tents, and only allowed large umbrellas or tiny tents — sometimes called bivvies — that will usually shelter a single angler. On the few occasions I've fished all night, I have a tendency to keep fishing, and it's not been a popular choice.

"Oi you, can you turn that light off? I'm trying to sleep over here!"

"Sorry. Just baiting up. Won't be a minute."

"WHAT?? You're not fishing are you? Of all the inconsiderate so-and-sos!"

The hammock is the perfect angler's tent — lightweight, comfortable and easy to put up. It doesn't even disturb the ground and gives you a great night's sleep.

Yes, to the bivouac, or bivvy, angler the fact that you might want to stay awake all night and actually fish is an alien concept that causes all sorts of problems. The notion that you are awake and alert while he is asleep and inert is faintly disturbing to our dome-dwelling friend, who prefers to approach fishing like a factory worker clocking on for the night shift, or maybe a fire fighter getting his head down for the night, but with one ear cocked for the sound of the siren.

Of course, the notion of a bivvy angler complaining to someone else about noise is hilarious in itself, given the fact that he typically arrives with air-raid-siren levels of electronic buzzers required to wake him from sleep — and that's before the clanking of all the pots and pans, the transistor radio, and the rumbling of the articulated cart he uses to carry everything in.

WEAPONS OF CHOICE

I've only ever fished with two rods once, and I couldn't stand the pressure of thinking what would happen if I got a bite on both of them at the same time. Carp, pike, catfish, and big eel anglers in particular seem to thrive on this pressure, and will often have three or sometimes even four baits in the water at the same time, scattered all over the lake. I couldn't cope.

Now, as I said before, I love to camp and I enjoy few things more than a night out under the stars. My weapon of choice for this kind of work is the Hennessy Hammock — an ultralight hammock and rainfly contraption that goes up in a couple of minutes, is comfier than any bedchair, and packs down so small I can almost fit it in the big back pocket of my vest. On really warm nights I don't even bother with a sleeping bag, but snuggle up in a blanket with my inflatable cushion for a pillow.

Thus equipped, I fish until I'm too tired to concentrate and then I reel in, pop the hook on the first eye of the rod, seal up all the bait, and then turn in and go to sleep. That way I wake at first light, when the fishing's likely to be as refreshed as I am, make a quick cup of tea, throw in some loose feed, cast out, and let the day begin anew.

FISHING IN THE FUTURE

So what does the next century hold for angling? Will it be marginalized or banned, or will the fish, sickened by pollution, simply fade away? Or will the future be even more fantastical than that? Fans of serious science fiction (or indeed of angling or science) should look away now.

As fish stocks fall and the cost of keeping waters clean enough to support them becomes prohibitively expensive, science will provide a low-cost alternative to real fish that keeps the sport alive and allows disillusioned anglers to flourish once more. Amazingly, it also keeps conservationists and abolitionists happy. I refer, of course, to robot fish.

Sound a bit fanciful? Not really. Mitsubishi designed an 88 lb. (40 kg.) cyber-Coelacanth in 2002 (they make that HR40 stuff that goes into fishing rods, so why shouldn't they make the fish as well?), while the Massachusetts Institute of Technology is already prototyping a robot pike. And visitors to the London Aquarium can already see three robot fish developed at Essex University. Best of all, Ryoumei Engineering in Japan has developed a gorgeous golden carp, three feet (90 cm.) long and, at 40 lb. (19 kg.), enough to make most European anglers wet themselves.

The idea of a computer-controlled robot fish isn't as daft as it sounds. Well, OK, maybe it is.

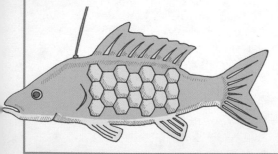

PERFECTING THE TECHNOLOGY

Having seemingly solved Gray's paradox (that fish don't have enough muscle power to propel themselves through the water at the speed they do), it's surely not beyond the wit of these clever-clogs eventually to reduce the astronomical cost of such metal monsters so that every angler can enjoy them. Each species (indeed, each individual fish) could be programmed with its own personality — Sony's AIBO robot dog already carries its personality on a tiny electronic card, about half the size of a stick of chewing gum.

The robot fish would know all about the snags in a particular stretch, could be programmed to ignore an angler's offerings at certain times of the day, come on the feed at others — and spend the cold winter months sheltering on the bottom of the lake or river buried in cyber-mud, a compound alive with nano-robots that would clean and service the fish ready for the spring. Robo-tiddlers would need very little processing power, making them a low-cost favorite, while larger fish could be customized to gigantic proportions and, with a memory upgrade or two, become quite uncatchable.

Unlike those who hunt them, such fish would grow wiser without ever aging, and they would mingle with the dwindling population of real fish who, over time, would come to revere them as gods. Problem solved.

BAITS YOU CAN BOTH EAT

Given that anglers are the most resourceful of sporting types, it's only natural that from time to time they improvise in order to catch their elusive quarry. In a sense, it's a variation on the ancient philosophical question: which came first, the angler's lunch or the bait? In my time, I've found it useful to bring along plenty of comestibles that can serve either purpose.

Anything with bread works well, so that's the entire sandwich pantheon at your disposal. Tough, long-lasting snacks like cheese are also winning baits, thanks in part to their strong smell. This is an enduring theme. We've already established that fish have a tremendous sense of smell (see page 70), so it should not be beyond the wit of an angler to roll bread paste around in a bag of cheese-and-onion crisps in order to give it a kick, or to observe that a paté sandwich is likely to be just as attractive to a large difficult-to-catch fish as a stick of spicy salami. Indeed, most greasy snacks can be pressed into service and I once caught a carp on bacon-flavor crisps that had been thoroughly masticated and then left to dry in the sun. Roach are partial to milk — but not plain — chocolate, carp enjoy bananas, and while I'm sure they'd eat it if they could, I've yet to find a way of getting yogurt to stay on the hook. But I haven't given up yet.

FISHING FROM THE TREES

I'd love to claim that this innovation was my own, but as far as I know, the honor belongs to two English angling eccentrics — Chris Yates and Bob James — who, while filming a sequence about carp fishing for a TV program, decided that the only way to catch a particularly large fish was to cast to it from the top of a tall tree. Inevitably, hilarity ensued.

Having hooked the fish, they were then forced to jump in and play it up to their waists in water. It was great fun. I used to watch it with my daughter, who was learning to talk. I would ask which video she wanted to watch and she would reply "Men jump in the water." She loved it to bits.

If you're fortunate enough to fish a water that's got good, strong trees round the edge, these can be an invaluable aid to finding what the fish are up to. You need patience and a head for heights (and a pair of binoculars), and I wouldn't recommend actually casting from the trees as Chris and Bob did, but over time you'll learn a tremendous amount about how fish use the lake — their feeding habits and patrolling patterns — and by dropping in the occasional piece of bait you can see how they react to it.

Taking advantage of such a bird's-eye view is not, it seems to me, unfair in the slightest. Should you use your brains in the pursuit of large fish, then hurrah for you and tough luck for the fish.

FREE-LINING

As we come to the end of the book, it's fitting that we should briefly consider the most basic fishing method of all — free-lining. Free-lining simply requires a rod, reel, line, hook, and bait, but no other end tackle, and is one of the most exciting and successful forms of fishing. It's also one of my favorite methods.

The benefits of free-lining are simple — with no terminal tackle on the end of your line apart from the hook and the bait, there's direct contact between you and the fish during the bite, strike, and fight itself. Of these, the bite is the most crucial. You should try casting a variety of different kinds of rigs into clear, shallow water so you can wade out and look at how they end up presenting the bait to the fish. You can set up your rigs as carefully as you like, but there'll still be twists and kinks that will undo all your work and make your bait stick out like a warning sign that keeps fish away rather than attracting them.

Nothing but the hook and the bait on the end of your line — fishing at its simplest.

There's much less chance of this when you're free-lining, and you'll also find that you get snagged less frequently and lose less tackle. But it's the sensitivity that most anglers enjoy — a direct line between you and the fish, like an electrical circuit that completes when the fish takes the bait, because when you're free-lining, you can feel every little bump and nibble from the shyest of fish. And when the fight is on, there's no large lead or whatever swinging around, whacking the fish on the nose every ten seconds.

The bait makes less sound when it hits the water, too. I know many anglers believe that the sound of a feeder packed with groundbait alongside a three-ounce lead will bring the head of every fish in the river up with curiosity, but I think that too much noise puts as many fish down as it attracts. Remember that fish are extremely sensitive to sound and use it as one of their main ways of seeking out food. Also remember that there's a difference between the sound of the dinner bell and someone banging an empty saucepan next to your ear.

Finally, when your fellow anglers (who are using the most expensive and sophisticated end tackle that money can buy) are biteless, there's the unmistakable sound of reverse one-upmanship, as your no-nonsense, back-to-basics approach comes up trumps with a stunning fish.

Dapping

One of the most effective ways of free-lining is to fish with a large insect on the surface of the water — a technique called dapping. Creep toward the edge, and when the rod is in position, release the bail arm and lower the bait gently onto the surface. If a fish does take the bait, it'll only be an arm's-length away.

THE LAST CAST

There will come a time when one simply stops fishing, when the faculties and senses grow too weak to enjoy it or the spirit that burns inside every angler just holds its hands up and says "enough." It's a day that will come to us all.

Will I know? I wonder, as I shuffle my way through the high ferns toward a nice flat spot above the sunken tree, where the river chuckles over a shallow gravel run before fanning out again into deeper water. Even a couple of years ago I might have tried to slide into the spot above that is more concealed and rarely fished, but since I had my other hip done I'm not sure I could get back up again, so it's another spot I won't be fishing any more, another "x" on the map.

I fish less and less often these days, sometimes because my daughter can't give me a lift, but more often because I don't relish it as much. And each trip I wonder — is this the last time I'll come to this spot, the last time I'll see the leaves turning here, the last time I'll bend down to make the chum that smells of strawberries, the last time I'll raise my hand in silent greeting to the angler on the opposite bank whose name I'll never know? I won't miss these cold mornings, that's for sure. Or the way my knees are stiff and sore for the first few hundred yards, or November's black ice and that bloody gate just where the path turns the corner.

Of course I will. I'm the man who loves everything about fishing. I'm the man who even loves packing up.

I ledger these days because the float is too difficult to see and the centerpin too fiddly to control, but that's no real hardship. I always preferred it as a technique and it always caught me bigger fish, though now I almost dread catching anything decent as it wears me out. I think about Zen angling some days — fishing without a bait, perhaps having a nice snooze in the sunshine.

Will I know? I wonder. Will it come in a moment of clarity on the bank as the sun disappears behind the trees, will it happen as I watch a fat fish swimming away while I wipe my hands on the old cloth, pleased as Punch; or will it come sitting in the parking lot waiting for my daughter to pick me up, not liking the look of the kids hanging around by the swings?

"Did you have a good time, Dad?"

"Yes thanks."

She gives my arm a little squeeze and we're off, and — suddenly — I know. Just like that. No fanfares, no final photograph freezing the moment forever in time. Although it was only minutes ago, I can't remember my last cast any more than I can remember my first, but I know that's it. I'm done.

INDEX

To mom and dad —
The boy, still fishing